*I found that the uncomfortable situations I was in
allowed me to grow the most.
The different skills and tools I learned
helped me to change for the better,
and I still implement them to this day.*

—*TJ*

A WILDERNESS JOURNEY

THE STORY OF A TEEN'S ROAD TO HEALING

TAMI ANN

Editor: Gina @ Killing It Write
Manuscript Editor: Elizabeth Slocum
Art Direction: Karen S. Blumé
Interior Illustrations: Elyse Whittaker-Paek
Book Layout: Gina Mansfield Design
Book Cover & Monomyth Design: Arash Jahani

ISBN# 978-0-578-33193-5

For the purpose of confidentiality,
names of people, locations, therapy programs,
and program details have been altered
to protect privacy.

Printed in the United States of America

to
My loving husband and journey companion
My special and talented daughter
My mom and dad
who love and support me unconditionally
And my son,
who took me on a winding path
that led to deep personal growth

TABLE OF CONTENTS

ACKNOWLEDGMENTS

First and foremost, I would like to say how grateful I am to my family and two dogs for being patient with me as I spent many hours hiding away while working on this project. When I began the writing process, I had no idea how much time I would spend sitting at my desk glued to my computer. (My back and rear end are still recovering!)

I am especially beholden to my husband, Tom, who has stuck by me all these years, took the wilderness journey with me, and rallied behind me as I brought this book to the finish line.

I have so much love and appreciation for my beautiful daughter who hung in there while her brother went through challenging times. I know it was not easy for her.

For my son, TJ, I applaud him for having the courage to allow me to bring his story to life so that we might help others. I admire him so much for wearing his heart on his sleeve.

A special thanks to my mom and dad for bringing me into this world, loving me unconditionally, and being my pillars throughout all my journeys in this life.

To my brother who gave me a thumbs up on everything I showed him regarding the book.

I love you all more than words can say.

A special thanks to my magnificent mentors: first off, my dad, who not only gave me constructive critiques as I slogged through the endless rough drafts but offered me a hand by using his magical Photoshop skills. (Thanks Dad, I love you!) To my incredible editors, Gina and Lizze, who were always available to lead me through rough patches and refine the story without taking away my voice. And last but not least, Gina M., my manuscript layout designer. She made the process of polishing and beautifying the book seem effortless.

An enormous thank you to my beta readers for your encouragement and for opening my eyes to different views: Mom, Dad, Nancy S., Mary Ann M., Susan F., Sherry S., Carolyn G., Stephanie F., Cherie D., Pam S., Marina M., Jessica G., Emily F., Maxine A., Anne M., Bill K., and John Q.

A shout-out to family and friends who put up with me emailing and text bombing for feedback on the cover artwork. (You know who you are!) I owe you all a big bear hug. Especially Elyse P., who also helped me to pull the story together with her beautiful illustrations.

I have so much appreciation for the professionals in the Outdoor Behavioral Healthcare and mental health fields who read the manuscript and provided their valuable guidance: first, I am truly grateful to Jonathan Mitchell, my son's mentor. He saw my vision for a book about Wilderness Therapy coming from a veteran parent and child's perspective. I feel deeply honored that he accepted my offer to write the foreword. A heartfelt thanks to educational consultants Dr. Teri Solochek and Scott Canter (The SC Group) and Talley Webb (Journey to Better) for pointing out key elements and offering their brilliant input. Many thanks to Dr. Mike Gass for the relevant contributions from his many decades worth of experience from the field of Adventure Therapy. I am much obliged to Dr. Will White for reading the preliminary version of the manuscript and educating me on Wilderness Therapy with his book and podcast. Thank you to Dr. Robert McCarron, UCI Professor of Psychiatry and Assistant Dean, CME, for his encouragement and constructive comments.

A hat tip for my wonderful support groups who have walked alongside me on this path. I've learned so much from our interactions and from hearing their empowering stories. These heroic parents sparked my inner drive to author this book.

Kudos to the wilderness heroes and their families who stepped out to share their letters and reflections from their outdoor therapy programs for the concluding chapter: Carrin, Tyler, Katie, and Hunter.

A special nod to friends I met through my son's wilderness program: Carolyn, Heather, Misty, Lisa, Steve, Deborah, Allyson, Pam, Becky, and Tom.

And finally, I am so grateful to my son's program and to all the individuals who work in the field of Outdoor Behavioral Therapy: researchers, directors, therapists, and field guides. Their tireless work to help young people with emotional challenges is incredibly honorable. Through this process, they taught our son important life skills that he will apply for the rest of his life.

I have so much gratitude.

Tami

FOREWORD

By Jonathan S. Mitchell, MA, LPC
Wilderness Therapist

Courage needs a new definition. Many of us think of courage as being brave, confident, fearless, and without a wavering of doubt. This could not be more untrue. Real courage is taking action despite the terror that wants to stop us. It is a step we take because we know it is right. The doubts, the fears, and the trepidation do not vanish when we take that step, but we move forward because something inside of us tells us so. We act because we must.

The heartbreaking choice to send one's child to a Wilderness Therapy program could not more fully embody this existential choice in a parent's life. The parent knows their child may be feeling furious, devastated, and potentially betrayed by the people in this world they've been trained to trust the most. Families often worry that their child will never forgive them for making this choice and never forget the depth of deception for extracting them from everything they know and sending them somewhere completely foreign. However, the parent who makes this choice knows (or perhaps only hopes) the child will ultimately return to the person that parent knew they always could be.

Tami and her husband, Tom, are two parents among thousands who have lived through this pivotal step. They knew their son needed help. TJ was lost, and they needed to get him back. Yes, he would likely be furious with them, feel utterly betrayed and abandoned by them, and likely feel like he was being kicked while he was down, but this did not stop them from doing what they knew was right. His potential was too great. He was too remarkable of a person for them to let him flounder any longer. Something had to be done. This is courage.

But not only did TJ's parents navigate this odyssey of Wilderness Therapy, Tami then chose to share it with the world. She is about to take you on a journey into the depths of a mother's love, a mother's heartbreak, a mother's desperate attempt to save her child's life. It is a raw, transparent experience of the Wilderness Therapy journey, one which touches upon every facet of transformation. You will see and feel their son's experience of betrayal, his fear of facing himself, his resistance to feeling and healing his own pain, and ultimately, the victory of self-actualization.

You may be a parent who has traversed this winding wilderness journey or may be considering this challenging choice. This book is also for you—to inform, to share, and to inspire. Wherever and whoever you may be, I invite you to open your mind and your heart to a story that pulls on the very fabric of the parent-child bond in the most unique of ways. A kind of tug that makes the bond simultaneously stronger and more transparent through its re-creation.

Tami pulls back the curtain on the Wilderness Therapy experience, as told through a parent willing to go beyond her own fear and doubts to save her child's life. And you will hear how her son shares his own perspective just as vulnerably as he walks the path of a student of Wilderness Therapy through the fire of his own transformation.

Jonathan S. Mitchell, MA, LPC
Durango, CO

LETTER FROM THE AUTHOR

Dear Fellow Parents,

I wrote this book for families who have either made or are considering making the gut-wrenching decision to place their struggling child in a Wilderness Therapy program. What you will discover among these pages is an honest and hopeful account of our family's journey toward healing, and one I would have wanted to read when searching for options to help my child.

For this narrative, I took the middle path. I am not necessarily promoting Wilderness Therapy for all children battling mental illness or substance abuse, or even debating its effectiveness. My purpose here is to share what I learned along the way, from one parent to another. My intent is to give an overview of what one might expect by sharing our son's chronicle, which happened to also be a parallel journey with his dad and me. I am also aware there is no promise or cure when you send your teen to a program in the wilderness and am mindful that my perspective is colored by our own successful experience.

For my son, Wilderness Therapy was a rewarding voyage toward personal enlightenment and emotional strength. I will highlight the route we took to prepare you for what may lie ahead for you and your child and to offer a story of hope.

Outdoor Behavioral Therapy was a last-resort treatment after years of trying local traditional resources. During the onset of adolescence, my now-former teenager was a danger to himself. He suffered from depression, anxiety, and ADHD, which led to drug use and suicidal ideation. His dad and I worried we would lose him if we did not find some way to put a stop to a potentially devastating derailment. He was on many different psychiatric medications and went to individual and family therapy at an outpatient Dialectical Behavior Therapy (DBT) program. He obtained IEP school supports and even changed high schools. Despite all these efforts, he became progressively worse. Our previously happy child was continuously self-medicating and sneaking out (and driving) with kids under the influence. While high and depressed, he even contemplated jumping off a high-rise building but was thankfully tackled by a security guard. Traditional therapy was a Band-Aid applied to a gushing wound. We needed to step it up and do something drastic to keep him safe.

While exploring different therapeutic options, I heard about this non-traditional outdoor mode of treatment through a friend. At first, it seemed to be a crazy and scary idea, simply because it entails dropping your child off in an uninhabited region for nearly three months, with the only means of communication being through weekly letters. To me, it sounded like child abandonment! But my husband and I were intrigued by it, so we hired an educational consultant (EC), a specialist in these kinds of therapeutic programs who is familiar with all the schools and facilities. She also matched our son with a specialized and seasoned therapist.

Positive changes finally happened after our son was removed from his toxic world and relocated to a place of natural wonder where he could break unhealthy patterns of behavior while working with a group of peers going through similar struggles. He made fire with sticks, hiked for miles on rough terrain with an enormous backpack, built a shelter with only a tarp and some ropes, and learned about natural consequences from Mother Nature. At the same time, his dad and I were at home, working hard to learn about our parental shortcomings.

Through grit and gumption, our son began to rely on himself and ultimately gained a new outlook on life. Although it was an agonizing decision to separate him from the family, and one that was not taken lightly, we are now thankful this opportunity was available.

You may wonder if our son *liked* Wilderness Therapy. The answer is not a definite yes or no. He vacillates from remembering moments of fun to recalling loathing it and then to admitting it was exactly what he needed. Looking back, he said, "I found that the uncomfortable situations I was in allowed me to grow the most. The different skills and tools I learned helped me to change for the better, and I still implement them to this day."

If you are reading this book because your child is beleaguered by emotional difficulties and is in need of the next level of care, I deeply sympathize with you. Not too long ago, I was standing in your shoes, so I can understand how you are feeling right now: stressed, worried, tired, and at the end of your rope. Your home environment may be out of control, and your family needs a drastic change for the better. If Outdoor Experiential Therapy is considered a proper treatment modality for your child by a mental health professional and you decide to follow this rocky but potentially rewarding road, know that you are not alone and that there is a road map. The trails have been well traveled by the heroes who have come before you.

Thank you for taking the journey with us.

—Tami Ann

@www.instagram.com/awildernessjourney

@www.facebook.com/awildernessjourneybook

*I invite you to read the *Afterword* to learn more about how this book evolved, the *Resources* to help you navigate the world of Outdoor Behavioral Therapy, and the *Endnotes* where you will find all the sources from my parent research on this subject.

INTRODUCTION

A WILDERNESS HERO'S JOURNEY OVERVIEW

The hero is escorted by his dad early in the morning to a quest in the Utah desert. Everything is taken away from this hero—home, friends, electronics, weed. It is a call to adventure to a special world. At first, he is outraged, confused, and sad. The hero refuses the call by sending furious text messages to his mom and dad but there is no choice for him. He has a mission to carry out.

Once he enters this strange and unfamiliar land, he is introduced to a therapist-mentor who encourages and guides him across the threshold. This mentor bestows upon him the tools he needs to endure the hardships of snowstorms, homesickness, and uncertainty. The tests and challenges he faces along the way give him super strength to enter the deepest cave, where he encounters his dragons.

Meanwhile, back at home, his mom and dad are taking their part in this journey by writing letters, reading assigned workbooks, and attending parent workshops to communicate on the same level as their son.

The hero makes fires with sticks, climbs mountains with a heavy backpack, and manages his dragons with skill. He begins to view the world he had first considered a "wasteland" as a breathtaking place with vivid colors. He becomes the leader of newly arrived heroes looking for guidance. After being rewarded with special recognition for seizing the treasure of emotional resilience, he returns to the ordinary world *triumphantly. This experience changes him. The hero outgrows his old life and is now ready for the next journey.*

A CALL TO ADVENTURE

Objectives of *A Wilderness Journey*

Our son, TJ, is the main character of this story, which makes him the hero. Although he did not know it at the time his voyage began, he was a hero of his own journey. His dad and I placed him in a Wilderness Therapy program in Utah to help him reset his life. TJ was grappling with emotional difficulties, and his problems resulted in a life-threatening situation. When he went to live in the wilderness, he left his comfort zone, achieved something that was beyond what he thought was ever possible, and returned home a changed person.

The purpose of this book is both to narrate our son's journey and illuminate Wilderness Therapy—also known as Outdoor Behavioral Health-care (OBH), Adventure Therapy, Outdoor Experiential Therapy, or "the woods"—to help other families understand the process. It is a guidebook of sorts, and a story all rolled into one. The story, which is mostly told with our letters and journals, will at times be interjected with information and parenting skills we learned along the way.

TJ's journey is not a particularly unique one because many other students of Wilderness Therapy have trod comparable paths. The details of each individual experience vary according to personalities and circumstances, but the same journey had been traveled *thousands and thousands* of times before him. The concluding chapter incorporates several other testimonials from teens who have undergone transformative changes through outdoor therapy. They have each taken a hero's journey.

The hero's journey, known as the *monomyth*, is a concept originally set forth in 1949 by famed scholar Joseph Campbell in his book *The Hero with a Thousand Faces*. Campbell's work is a comparative study of how the same underlying structure exists in myths, legends, and folklore. There are three main phases to the monomyth: separation, initiation, and return. The following story of my son's outdoor therapy experience was woven together using the hero's journey as a framework. It is a tailored version derived from the Disney screenwriter Christopher Vogler's rendition of the hero's journey for his book *The Writer's Journey: Mythic Structure for Writers*.

THE HERO'S JOURNEY

SEPARATION
Ordinary World
Call to Adventure
Refusal of the Call
Meeting with the Mentor

INITIATION
Crossing the First Threshold
Tests, Allies, Enemies
Approach to the Inmost Cave
Ordeal

RETURN
Reward (Seizing the Sword)
The Road Back
Resurrection
Return with the Elixir

The steps in this hero's journey sequence above have been inspired by Christopher Vogler for his book *The Writer's Journey: Mythic Structure for Writers*.

Joseph Campbell's philosophy has influenced screenwriters and authors of all different genres. One of the best-known examples of the hero's journey in a movie is in *Star Wars*. The original film begins with Luke Skywalker living on a moisture farm in outer space with his aunt and uncle. Obi-Wan Kenobi calls him on a quest to destroy the evil Empire. At first, Luke refuses the call but eventually agrees to *separate* from his ordinary life and cross the threshold. He is *initiated* into a world full of obstacles as a Jedi warrior as his mentors, Obi-Wan Kenobi and Yoda, train him to conquer the enemies. When Luke *returns* home, he is celebrated as a hero, bringing freedom and new hope to the galaxy.

The hero's journey not only underlies fictional stories but also reflects every human experience. Adopting a pet, starting a new career, giving birth, or facing health issues are a few examples. These life events all begin with a call for change that arrives with a set of challenges. We meet mentors (dog trainers, friends, teachers, co-workers, doctors) who guide us through the road blocks. In the end, we resurface as wiser and empowered versions of ourselves.

Wilderness Therapy is often compared to the hero's journey by professionals in the field. It is a therapeutic intervention for emotionally struggling youth in which they are separated from their families to stabilize and work on finding the root cause of emotional issues so they can heal and grow. It is an immersive environment where relationship and problem-solving skills are practiced 24/7 while working with a team of licensed mental health professionals. Students learn hard and soft skills. Hard, meaning survival techniques such as building shelter, making fires, cooking their own food, and staying comfortable in the elements. And soft, meaning communication skills, gratitude, and doing deep therapeutic work. The heroes arrive as underdogs and are matched with a student mentor. As time goes on, they move up the ranks and become mentors themselves, which is a crucial element in the journey. Mentors feel a sense of pride and accomplishment in being able to teach the difficult skills they have mastered.

It is a stressful and terrifying experience for parents to drop their child off in unfamiliar places with unfamiliar people. The family may be skeptical and resistant because this sojourn will require change, and change is difficult. Yet, if parents understand that there is a trajectory their children will go through in Wilderness Therapy that generally follows the sequence of the hero's journey, the fear of seeking this type of help for their children could be minimized.

At the front end of the wilderness journey, I was given advice from other parents whose children had completed outdoor therapy programs; that advice was to "trust the process." This phrase did not put me at ease because I was petrified to take my son out of high school, away from the comforts of home, and place him in the mountains with strangers—for twelve weeks! Instead of trusting the process, I now know it would have been much better for us if we *understood the process*.

To help you visualize what a typical wilderness journey might look like, follow the circular path of the adapted *Wilderness Hero's Journey Monomyth*.

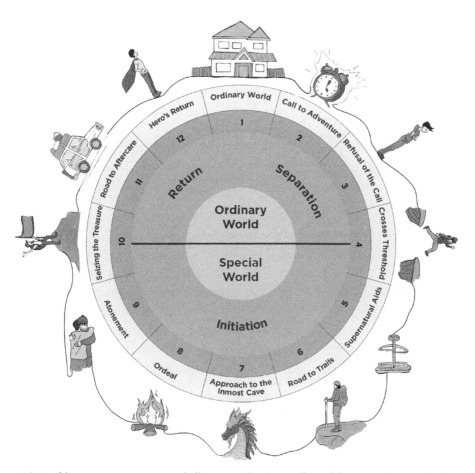

The Wilderness Journey Monomyth illustration has been adapted from Joseph Campbell's hero's journey in his book *The Hero with a Thousand Faces*. According to Wikipedia (*https://en.wikipedia.org/wiki/Hero%27s_journey*), "The monomyth is the common template of stories that involve a hero who goes on an adventure, is victorious in a decisive crisis, and comes home changed or transformed."

Starting at the top of the wheel, the hero begins the journey at home in the **ordinary world (1)**, then progresses clockwise through the steps of the circle. They are **called to adventure (2)** but will likely **refuse the call (3)** by sending "rescue me" letters from the field to the family. Heartbreaking messages negotiating to come home, which may be laced with F-bombs, are a common form of refusal. They **cross the threshold (4)** to the *special* *world* and acquire **supernatural aids** (5), or tools, to serve them on this journey. They venture on the **road of trials** (6) and endure a series of tests and challenges. When they **approach the inmost cave** (7), the hero faces their dragons and navigates through a succession of **ordeals** (8). Next, there is a possibility for them to **atone** (9) with the family during a visit to their special world. After completion of the wilderness program, they **seize the treasure** (10) and leave the woods on the **road to aftercare** (11) in the *ordinary world* where they re-enter society with running water and electricity. Finally, the **hero returns home** (12) to complete the journey.

My son was amused and thought it was funny when I told him I was casting him as a hero in the story. If you knew what he was like leading up to Wilderness Therapy, "hero" would not be a term you would use to describe him, because his behaviors were not much like those of a hero you would imagine in a movie or storybook. But being a hero does not mean you need to have superhuman strength, be able to control lightning, or become the greatest Jedi the galaxy has ever known. It can also mean having the guts to step out of regular life and into the unknown world to achieve personal strength and enlightenment.

Students in Outdoor Behavioral Therapy programs are not the only ones on the journey; parents and caregivers become heroes on a journey of their own as well. What is critical to success is understanding that kids cannot be delivered to the wilderness to be "fixed." Families also need to do the work to make changes within themselves, so when their child returns, they will not fall back on ineffective communication patterns. While our son went on his healing adventure, his dad and I worked alongside him from afar. We may not have made fire with sticks for warmth or slumbered under a tarp for months in the rain and snow, but we traveled simultaneously with him while connecting through therapeutic assignments, letters, field visits, and at his graduation ceremony. We transformed through a physical and mental process of separating from each other, working to improve ourselves, and then reconnecting with a new set of communication and emotional regulation skills. It is a parent-child parallel process.

One of the many things I learned on this road to recovery was that Wilderness Therapy is not considered to be the last step in a treatment journey but a component of a long-term plan. It came as a surprise to me at first because three months seemed like a long time for my child to be away from home. At the same time, I had to remind myself that it took many *years* for my son to get to the unhealthy place he was in before he left. Words to describe Wilderness Therapy are "reset," "launchpad," or "intervention." Following the outdoor program, our seventeen-year-old went straight to a therapeutic boarding school, where he graduated from high school. He then moved to a sober living program near his college for another year, where he embraced AA, and is currently studying computer engineering.

Of all the interventions we attempted, Wilderness Therapy was the key that unlocked the change our son so desperately needed. For this reason, our story will be focusing on this aspect of his long therapeutic journey, because it was the most profound stepping stone for him.

Placing a child in wilderness is heart-wrenching, empowering, challenging, and ultimately life-changing. It is a type of treatment you cannot find anywhere else; not in an office building, intensive outpatient program, psychiatric hospital setting, or on a Zoom call, and certainly not at home. The wilderness alone is therapeutic and, when combined with behavior therapy techniques, it can be incredibly powerful. While every child has distinct reasons for being there, each one shares several traits: being at-risk and crying for help. Their paths reflect the monomyth to an amazing degree.

I invite you to take an intimate peek into our son's call to adventure, which was also a parallel journey as we learned how to speak more effectively with each other and how to connect on a deeper level. This is the story of a teen's (and a family's) road to healing.

Primary Sources for *A Wilderness Journey*:

- *The Hero with a Thousand Faces*, by Joseph Campbell (1949).

- Handpicked letters, select field journals excerpts, and post reflections from a teenage boy's Wilderness Therapy-to-aftercare experience.

- Feelings, observations, and research of a Wilderness Therapy-to-aftercare journey from a mother's perspective.

Other Particulars About This Book:

- This is a true story. The names of family members, my son's peers, and the wilderness field staff were changed to protect privacy.

- For the purpose of confidentiality, the names of my son's Wilderness Therapy program and aftercare remain anonymous. Additionally, locations and programing details of these therapeutic facilities have been altered.

- In the *Afterword*, you will learn about out how a stack of earth-smudged handwritten letters and journals from a wilderness journey became a book.

- The *Research*, *Resources*, and *Glossary* at the end of the story contain information to help families navigate Wilderness Therapy: parent research, recommended books and podcasts, ways to pay for outdoor therapy, support organizations, and terminology.

- Refer to the *Endnotes* for citations on the books, websites, journals, and videos I found helpful on the topic of the hero's journey, mental health, and Outdoor Behavioral Healthcare.

A WILDERNESS
JOURNEY

PHASE I: SEPARATION

What I think is that a good life is one hero journey after another. Over and over again, you are called to the realm of adventure, you are called to new horizons. Each time, there is the same problem: do I dare? And then if you do dare, the dangers are there, and the help also, and the fulfillment or the fiasco. There's always the possibility of a fiasco.

But there's also the possibility of bliss.

—Joseph Campbell, *Pathways to Bliss*

CHAPTER 1

ORDINARY WORLD

THE WILDERNESS HERO

Once upon a time, there was an all-American boy named TJ who resided in the ordinary world *of Suburbia. He lived in the same house with his two loving parents from the day he was born and had a goodhearted younger sister named Beth. The family adopted a scruffy white dog whom they called Tango because of how he tap-danced with his front paws to vie for their attention. TJ's dad, Tom, worked long hours to support the family at an office close to home, while his mom, Tami, managed the family affairs, home-schooled his sister, and volunteered on the school board. Life for TJ could not be more ordinary.*

Picture a six-foot-tall, lanky teen with a mop of wavy chestnut hair who liked wearing distressed jeans with holes in the knees. While attending the local public high school, he played a few sports and went skateboarding and surfing in his free time. If he was not spending late nights composing music on his Logic Pro program and dreaming of becoming a producer, he was out with friends, getting high.

This world might not seem ordinary for some, but it was the place of origin before TJ embarked on a journey to the special world *of a Wilderness Therapy program in Utah, where he would travel on a journey as a hero. It all began on a cold February morning in 2018 when TJ was removed from the comforts of home to become a little seed dropped onto desert soil. The location was in a remote area of the Four Corners region, where the hero was welcomed by kindly strangers and a campfire on a blustery winter evening.*

You may ask why this boy's mom and dad would make such a dramatic and drastic decision to separate their teenage son from his seemingly safe home life, right in the middle of his junior year of high school. The answer to that question is simple: he was on a reckless path, and his life was at risk. But before this story begins, you must first understand the situation at home.

What Led to Wilderness Therapy?

I am the proud mother of the hero in this story as my son climbed mountains in the wilderness, literally and figuratively. But before the ascent to the summit, TJ's life was spiraling on a downhill trajectory.

When he was about thirteen years old, one would say TJ was a typical kid, with all the qualities you'd think would lead him to become a well-adjusted, successful grown-up. However, once he transitioned to his teens, something was not right. The sweet, carefree boy we knew began showing signs of depression and anxiety. He became buried in dark clouds, isolating himself in his room. TJ was a compassionate and sensitive soul, yet he became quick to anger. He went from being MVP of the freshman water polo team and participating in the choir to falling behind in school and walking around with this blank look in his eyes. The coping mechanisms he used to make himself feel better created tremendous tension at home and in the world around him.

TJ's dad and I were not always sure how to respond to our son's mood swings, and we would discount them as typical adolescent behavior. But deep down, his dad and I knew this was not the average teen angst. We began collecting any information we could on helping a child with depression: books, podcasts, TED Talks, YouTube videos, and online articles.

I found my son's depression and anxiety to be frustrating and frightening. It was my job to make him better, but I did not know how to fix him. Even though I was aware depression was a chemical imbalance in his brain, I would still fall back on wondering how on earth he could be so sad when he had seemingly everything to grow up well adjusted, with a supportive family, a nurturing home environment, loving grandparents who were close by, and no traumatic events thus far in his life. But what we provided was not enough. There was an invisible psychological condition lurking inside him, causing a great amount of pain. I wanted to be the one to remedy it with a hug or a Band-Aid, but unfortunately it was not that simple.

When it comes to mental illness, the root cause is hidden from the world, no matter how abundantly visible the symptoms are. It's a lonely place to be, for family members as well, because your child's behavior causes you to put the blame on your parenting skills. This causes shame, which in turn causes you to remove yourself from the parent network around you. When someone has a broken leg, diabetes, or cancer, the condition garners much sympathy and support from the community. But who would send flowers or set up meal trains for families of kids with declining school performance, drug abuse, and suicidal ideation? These kids are only subjects of judgment, gossip, and avoidance. I felt the need to protect my son's privacy and was isolated because of it. I did not think anyone would understand what I was going through. All the other parents seemed solely concerned about their kids' grades, SAT scores, and college applications.

During this tumultuous time with TJ, I began writing about what was happening in a little brown leather journal. My diary became my best friend. Not only did it help me keep track of the events, but it was also a great healing tool, providing a place to anchor my thoughts around the emotional distress.

Depression, Anxiety, Attention Difficulties, Substance Abuse, Suicidal Ideation

The adolescent mental health crisis has been growing in epidemic proportions over the past decade. It is difficult to pinpoint a specific reason, but it's most likely a combination of genetics and environmental factors such as social media, pressure to succeed, and poor coping mechanisms. Our son was no exception and was becoming a victim of this so-called epidemic. We were grasping at straws as we tried a variety of different local resources to help him.

Local Traditional Therapy Attempted

Talk Therapy: Cognitive Behavior & Dialectical Behavior Therapy

When TJ was thirteen, we were referred to a cognitive behavioral therapist (CBT) in the local area and began weekly individual therapy sessions. The psychologist we found was a good fit, and the regular visits seemed to be going well for a while. It was fortunate TJ felt comfortable opening up and sharing his feelings with the therapist, because that's when we learned he was drinking cough syrup. This news was a devastating blow. Tom and I had TJ sign a home contract promising he would stop ingesting the over-the-counter medication. We hoped he would take it seriously. But our pleas and the signed contract didn't make any difference to TJ, and the next thing we knew, there were large bottles of vodka in his desk drawers.

Realizing once-a-week therapy was not going to cut it, I found a local comprehensive outpatient program employing Dialectical Behavior Therapy (DBT) along with individual and family therapy. Tom and I were in a negative cycle of reactive parenting and needed help managing our emotions around what was going on. We had always thought we were easygoing and reasonable parents, but responding to a depressed, anxious, drug-abusing teen brought out the worst in us. With the DBT training, we learned emotional regulation skills, how to be better listeners, and how to validate feelings. We did the homework assignments in the *DBT®️ Skills Training Handouts and Worksheets* book by Marsha M. Linehan. It was our first encounter with *I-feel* statements, a powerful communication tool to preempt defensive reactions.

Psychiatric Medication

When TJ was entering ninth grade, we went down the rabbit hole of pharmaceuticals. I was optimistic that a psychiatrist would prescribe him a pill and his dark feelings would disappear. We soon realized it's more complex than that. The combination of medications prescribed for TJ's depression, attention deficit, and sleeplessness made him feel like he was living in the story of *Alice in Wonderland*.

The first chemical experiment was mostly a guess. TJ's psychiatrist chose Wellbutrin, a common norepinephrine-dopamine reuptake inhibitor (NDRI). After a few months, when we found that it did not lift TJ's mood, the doctor recommended a genetic test called Gene-Sight Psychotropic to help find a more effective medication. The gene test analyzes clinically important genetic variations in a person's DNA and tells how the body metabolizes or responds to antidepressant medications or SSRIs. The results were categorized in a color-coded report: green, yellow, and red. Using the information provided, the psychiatrist decided on a medication in the green category: Zoloft, a common SSRI antidepressant. When we learned that in some cases a side effect could be suicidal ideation, it seemed contradictory and concerning. Nevertheless, we were desperate enough to give it a try and of course hoped that suicidal ideation would not ensue for TJ. In addition, the doctor prescribed Gabapentin for treatment of TJ's insomnia and Adderall for his attention difficulties.

Waiting and wondering if the medications were the right fit was excruciating because it could take many weeks to determine the results. Below is a conversation between TJ and his dad, which was recorded outside our house with a Nest Cam when TJ was caught sneaking out at 2 a.m. on a school night. This exchange gives a picture of the frustrations of what it was like to experiment with pharmaceuticals and our son's brain chemistry, and how our hands were tied as we held our breath:

>TJ: "The medicine is not fucking working!"

>Dad: "Well, we haven't switched it yet. You have to go down on the current one."

>TJ: "You know if this doesn't work ..."

>Dad: "It won't be like you take a pill, and one day everything will be instantly fine. It will take a little time, okay?"

>TJ: "If this next pill doesn't work, I don't know what I'm going to do."

Dad: "If it doesn't work, we'll try something else. And the other thing is that you're growing a lot, and the chemistry in your body and brain is changing, so in six months, you may feel better."

TJ: "I don't know how I'll deal with the next six months. The bad feeling keeps coming in waves, and it keeps getting worse and worse, and that's when I take cough syrup. And now I don't have that, so I replaced it with going out in the middle of the night. If I can't go out, then what am I going to do? I don't know what I'm going to do!"

Dad: "When you talk with Dr. J, does he give you any suggestions or coping mechanisms?"

TJ: "We were talking about this today ... He said he'll teach me some next week.

Dad: So, next week ...(inaudible)"

TJ: "If I don't have an outlet, I don't know what I'm going to do."

Dad: "A lot of people use exercise as an outlet. What about lifting weights?"

TJ: "I need a better outlet than lifting weights. Cough syrup and going out at night works for me."

Dad: "Cough syrup will just make your problems worse, TJ."

TJ: "But this is the only thing that helps ..."

We experimented with several more antidepressants, to no avail. The meds resulted in complete dysregulation of TJ's emotions. The listed suicidal side effects did not turn out to be a myth, and our fears and doubts were validated. We hid the knives in the house and locked up all the medication. There were nights I slept on the floor next to TJ's bed when he seemed to be in danger of harming himself. Even his faithful dog, Tango, would cuddle up next to TJ in his bed when he sensed something was wrong.

Then I received an alarming call one night from TJ's friend's mother, who alerted me that TJ was talking about suicide to her son. The friend convinced TJ to call the suicide hotline. There were also several incidents when TJ stormed out of the house, leading us to believe his safety was at risk. On one particular night, we had police and a helicopter team searching for him.

Individualized Education Program (IEP) & Changing to a Private School

TJ's school performance plummeted during his freshman year. He would doze off in class after restless nights of sleep, or let his anxiety get to him so much that he could not follow through with assignments. We were advised by the school counselor to go through the process of obtaining an Individualized Education Program (IEP) to allow for accommodations at school to ease the pressure. The IEP is a legal document developed for eligible public-school students. It is a road map to help kids who need extra support to thrive in school.

The school agreed there was a need to perform a formal evaluation. Testing confirmed what we already knew: TJ had low executive functioning skills, anxiety, depression, and attention difficulties. We met with the IEP team, which included teachers, the academic counselor, school psychologist, and school administrators, to put together a plan to accommodate TJ's needs. He was granted extended time on tests or assignments, attended study skills classes and met regularly with the school psychologist. The IEP was helpful to a certain extent but not enough to fix the deep problems brewing inside our kid.

During the first week of TJ's sophomore year, he asked to switch to a private school where he knew a few friends from earlier in his childhood. Changing environments would give him a fresh start, we all hoped. Since it was too late for the fall semester, we jumped through hoops to make the change happen in spring. TJ's grades were inadequate, but the admissions officer said they would consider opening a spot if TJ checked a few boxes. He had to retake failed classes in addition to his full load at school, which caused a lot of anxiety, but he managed to get through it and be admitted. Things were looking up at the new school; that is, until we realized he had discovered a new set of friends who were poor influences. His social life eventually centered around cannabis in all forms: vaping and smoking high-potency marijuana wax, as well as other experimentations.

Self-medication

Although the DBT therapy was helpful to our family, weed was dominating TJ's behavior. He was convinced that smoking and vaping cannabis was the answer to all his problems. Drifting toward kids with access to substances, he established his place among the drug users at his school. TJ relentlessly attempted to convince us that weed made him a wizard at math and remedied his "back pain." The legalization of cannabis in California normalized the drug in his mind. He thought since it was now legal, how could it be bad? He would say to us, "It's a medicinal herb!" Or "It's no big deal, *all* of the kids do it!" Weed shops were popping up all over town, and even though you must be twenty-one years of age to buy it, it was easy for him to get a hold of it. I discovered shipments of weed were being delivered to our front yard bushes by dealers TJ had met at school or on social media. I found homemade pipes made with straws, pens, and plastic bottles around the house and discovered vape cartridges in his pockets when doing the laundry.

TJ's dad and I would try to chalk it up to teen experimentation and say to each other, "Well, at least it's only marijuana." But we also learned more about today's marijuana, which comes in much higher-concentrated versions. I spent hours researching how weed affects the young brain and printed out information for TJ to read, hoping that the facts would set him straight. But then TJ would find research in favor of using weed. He was deeply knowledgeable on the subject and had excellent arguments based on his extensive internet research. He asked to go off his antidepressants and smoke weed instead. He had a good point since the pharmaceutical antidepressants had been unsuccessful for him. I briefly considered a medical marijuana license and explored the shops to learn more about it. I asked TJ's psychiatrist if it would be a suitable alternative to administer to him controlled amounts of medical marijuana.

The doctor vehemently advised against it because he felt it was not regulated enough to be administered to teens while their brains are still developing. Studies show that exposure at an early age to tetrahydrocannabinol (THC), the main psychoactive ingredient in weed, can cause delayed maturation and trigger psychosis and schizophrenia when taken in higher doses.

TJ's argument was that weed is not addictive. It may not be as addictive as other drugs but, as I learned, regular cannabis consumption does incite a form of addiction. Scientific findings show that heavy marijuana use (or cannabis use disorder) is associated with the brain's reduced production of its own endocannabinoid neurotransmitters, causing the need to continue using cannabis to make up for the deficit, which in turn causes a continued cycle of dependency. During my online research, I stumbled across an illustrative analogy to weed dependence, told by a retired construction worker to another addict minimizing marijuana abuse:

Imagine an addict as a house. The addiction to "hard drugs" is like a bulldozer that, in a short amount of time, can destroy the house. It is loud and obvious. The house is now in pieces and must be rebuilt. Now imagine marijuana addiction as a termite infestation. Nobody notices one or two or even hundreds of termites. But after decades of growing in number, quiet and hidden, the house is now overrun, and the damage is irreversible.

It did not take long to become turned off to the idea of medicinal cannabis, but we wanted so badly for TJ to find something to alleviate his depression and anxiety. To give you an idea what he was feeling like during the time before wilderness, I have included a passage from his junior year chemistry notebook I discovered when cleaning out a drawer after he'd finished treatment. He had written it in between his notes on chemical formulas.

TJ: So today I had a good breakfast. I ate some waffles and bananas. I got into the car with Mom, and it was going well until she said something about the schedule in a way that made it seem like she was blaming me for something out of my control. I understand she was just observing something about the schedule, but whenever she does that, I feel like she's complaining about something I can't do anything about. Which usually makes me feel like I'm in a situation I can't control. It bothers me deeply if I feel like I'm not in control. It causes my anxiety to increase to a point of exhaustion, and unfortunately, due to my brain chemistry and methodical state, my brain clutters, and it becomes harder to use the validation skills that I know how to use. My brain works in mysterious ways. My thoughts are often hectic, while my body and exterior housing generally have a calm, observant façade. I feel like an observer not from this world, watching over another society that never slows down. Sometimes, I interact with the civilians, but that leads me to become more unsettled.

Home Contracts and Drug Testing

As TJ's substance abuse was ramping up, his dad and I would set forth ultimatums. We offered him chances to quit on his own or go to treatment. We drew up a home contract and had him agree to regular drug testing. Because THC stays in the system for at least thirty days, I took him to the lab every week to see if the numbers went down. Drug testing brought about a disconnect in our relationship because it showed a lack of trust, which was becoming a theme in our house.

It was uncomfortable being with TJ in the laboratory waiting for him to be tested as he sat there fuming. I kept wondering how it had come to this. Another problem with drug testing is that it caused him to become crafty in finding new ways to self-medicate right under our noses. TJ discovered drugs that did not show up on the tests, such as plants called kratom and salvia. I read a scary story once that a teenage boy died from "huffing" computer duster cans because his dad was testing him for marijuana, and duster inhalants do not show up on tests. This had me worrying that we were going to drive TJ toward something more dangerous.

Texts Between TJ and Me After a Positive Drug Test

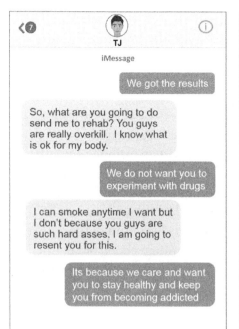

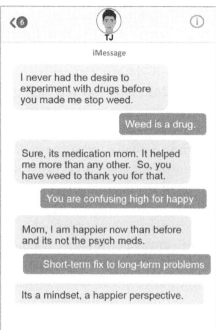

Termination of Therapist Due to Substance Use

Shortly before TJ turned seventeen, DBT therapy came to a halt when his therapist said she could no longer help him anymore because he was using substances to cope with his feelings instead of DBT skills. If TJ was choosing to get high, she said, she was not able to continue treatment. This was the beginning of Tom's and my realization that things were not going to get any better unless we removed him from his toxic world to get him the help he needed. My neighbor and dear friend Stephanie, who knew TJ was struggling, mentioned something to me about wilderness programs and how she happened to have had a friend whose son had gone to one. She suggested I consider this type of out-of-home placement. I subsequently asked both TJ's therapist and psychiatrist what they thought about enrolling him in an outdoor therapeutic environment, or even a therapeutic boarding school, but neither of them felt comfortable recommending them. I found out later that most local professionals have a negative image or limited understanding of therapy outside of four walls, often based on long-outdated information.

We were running out of time and running out of ideas. I could not stand by and watch TJ fall apart. His sister was traumatized by witnessing her brother's behaviors. We could not have rational conversations with him and felt like we were losing him to addiction. *My son was becoming an addict!* Those words were hard to say. And all I could ask myself was, *How did this happen?*

We needed to move fast, but where to turn now? We believed we had utilized every local resource to help him, and nothing was working. TJ needed a drastic change. We did not want to wait until he needed to be hospitalized for a drug overdose, suicide attempt, or a drunk driving incident.

My friend Stephanie, who I consider my guardian angel to this day, came to my rescue by recommending her educational consultant (EC). I had never heard of ECs before she explained what their role was to me, and I am grateful that she pointed me in the right direction with a seasoned and competent referral. I picked up the phone right away and called the number.

TJ's familiar world is about to be disrupted by a call to adventure.

CHAPTER 2

CALL TO ADVENTURE

The call to adventure separates the hero from his familiar life at home and places him in a new and special world where trials, tribulations, and triumphs await.

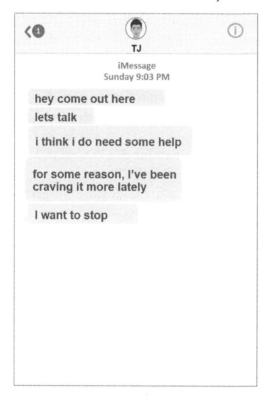

This was a text message TJ sent to his dad months before he went to the wilderness.

It was a call for help.

Mom's Narration:

Meeting the Mentor: The Educational Consultant

An educational consultant named Teri Solochek of The SC Group became the first mentor in our wilderness journey. She is a doctor of clinical psychology and a certified educational planner who helped us find the best-fitting program to align with TJ's needs.

To help Teri understand the full picture of what was going on with our son, we provided her a written summary of TJ's situation, mental health records, lists of medications, school records, and IEP testing. We signed authorization for disclosure forms for her to speak to each of his therapists and his psychiatrist. Once Teri had the full scope of TJ's story, she recommended Wilderness Therapy—also referred to as Outdoor Behavioral Healthcare, Adventure Therapy, Outdoor Experiential Therapy, or "the woods"—as a first step. Even though I had read about Wilderness Therapy during my online research, the thought of sending our son off to "the woods" for three months during his junior year of high school seemed too extreme. How would he finish high school? Shouldn't we wait until summer for this kind of thing? We asked Teri if it would make more sense to enroll TJ in a therapeutic boarding school so he would not fall behind in his academics. She gently reminded us of something we already knew: school is second to mental health. Our son would be more apt to absorb academics once he was emotionally regulated. Regardless of this, my head was spinning from the idea of TJ being in no man's land for so long.

As we hemmed and hawed considering Wilderness Therapy, Tom and I asked ourselves so many questions ... Would he ever forgive us? Would we look like bad parents? Are these programs abusive? Would he learn about new kinds of drugs and other risky behaviors?

An added cause for concern stemmed from reading online reviews and stories from advocacy groups, or "survivors" of the "troubled teen industry" who spread word about abusive programs. Teri warned us not to read online comments and social media posts because they can be misleading. Reviews are subjective, and the self-selected individuals who write them do not report typical experiences. Also, many former students' experiences took place more than ten years ago; there have been positive changes made in wilderness programs over the last decade or so. Teri assured us the programs she was choosing for TJ were compassionate, well respected, and comply with established best practices for safety and treatment. Additionally, she believed in choosing ones that incorporate a family systems approach. It is a form of therapy that considers family dynamics as an important piece of the puzzle when treating the child. An increasing number of wilderness programs are putting a strong emphasis on this key element because they are finding that it is crucial to success of their clients.

Teri winnowed it down to two outdoor programs for us to choose from based on the availability of the therapists she thought would be a good fit for TJ. It was a difficult choice, but we finally decided to put a stake in the ground, and Teri went forward with the arrangements.

When I broke the news of our plans to my mother and father, they were simply shocked. Our son is close to his grandparents. They had no idea how much detail we had been shielding from them about what had been going on. We usually gave them a fairy-tale version of things. They desperately suggested letting him move in with them instead of sending him away. Their offer was generous, but we politely declined, knowing the extent of the help TJ needed.

It happened to be the month of December when all this planning for TJ was occurring. The timing brought doubts because it seemed heartless to have our son sleep on the ground in the snow and live with people he didn't know during the holidays. The last time I checked the weather in Utah, it was blizzarding. There would be an empty place at the table on Christmas. But I knew the festivities wouldn't have much meaning with TJ in such a terrible state. So, we continued the enrollment process.

Meanwhile, the fact that the holidays were inching closer, combined with my parents' dismay over our plans, and TJ was somehow magically behaving better, fueled my doubts. He even wanted to help decorate the Christmas tree with the family. Maybe the meds and therapy were kicking in, or maybe we were putting our heads in the sand? I conveniently forgot about the previous Christmas when TJ stormed off and went missing the whole evening, only to stumble home bruised and bloodied after passing out and falling from a tree in an empty, unlit park.

So, I ignored the past, dug in my heels, and *refused the call*. Tom had been second-guessing our decision, so it did not take much convincing to sway him toward pulling the plug on this crazy therapy-in-the-woods idea.

In a state of panic, I found every reason to walk away, and I confessed to Teri we were scrapping the mission. Parents changing their minds must be a common occurrence, because she was not surprised to hear that we were backing out. Teri understood and knew we needed to be ready, but she also warned us that options could change as TJ approached his eighteenth birthday. Once he was of legal age, we would lose control over making his medical treatment decisions. I took note of her advice.

Meanwhile, the holidays came and went. To spare the details and make a long story short, there was a hair-raising New Year's Eve when we found videos on TJ's iPhone of him smoking out of bongs in a car full of kids who were also smoking, including the driver, followed by a few more months of ups and downs, and then a last straw that prompted my husband to finally say, "That's it! Call Teri. We are going to do this thing." I was still in denial and fell into shock hearing those words come from Tom's mouth. But without further hesitation, I went on autopilot and called Teri. She started searching again for more openings at several other Outdoor Behavioral Therapy programs with a proper therapist for TJ. In less than a week, we had an enrollment date set up in Utah. I had needed that push. This was our true call to adventure.

(Refer to the Resources *for more information on independent educational consultant associations and trade organizations that hold programs accountable for safe practices.)*

Mom's Journal:

Six Days Before Departure: Family Birthday Party for TJ

Sunday, 2/18/18
Last night we celebrated TJ's seventeenth birthday with extended family at our favorite Mexican restaurant. I organized the small party so they could see him one last time before he leaves. There was so much guilt built up in me for acting like everything was status quo. I felt a deep sadness as I watched him pose for pictures wearing a sombrero on his head. TJ had no idea the world he knew was about to be ripped out from under him.

Everyone was in on the secret except for the younger cousins. Although we all felt this underlying gloom, we put on our happy faces. I could see TJ was not enjoying himself. Not because he sensed what plans lay ahead, but because this was how he usually was during family occasions. Distant, withdrawn, and wanting to be somewhere else other than with us. He left the table a few times to make calls and texts to friends, or a dealer, I presumed.

Two Days Before Departure: TJ's Birthday

Wednesday, 2/21/18
The family celebrated TJ's real birthday on a school night at a luxury movie theater. Before we left the house, TJ said he was unsure if he should go because he had too much homework. We told him he could take a pass since it's his birthday. Unbeknownst to him, completing history and algebra assignments would be unnecessary in about thirty-six hours.

While lounging in comfortable reclining chairs, we were served dinner, popcorn, and drinks as we watched *Black Panther*. I couldn't pay attention to the movie. My mind was making up its own stories and thinking about how, in two days, TJ will be reclining on logs, dirt, and rocks.

Eve of Departure: Preparation

Thursday, 2/22/18

The past few days before transport have felt agonizingly long, and it's been hard to keep up with this charade of pretending everything is normal. I'm a miserable actor, so I'm somewhat relieved I don't have to pretend for much longer. Tomorrow is the big day.

The reality of what we are doing is starting to settle in. Planning TJ's enrollment has kept my mind occupied for the past week, which allowed me to avoid my true emotions. But tonight, I lost it. I couldn't go into the house after coming home from the market to buy special snacks for Tom and TJ's flight. I sat there in the car, in complete darkness and silence, parked in the front driveway, mulling over everything that was about to take place. Primarily, it dawned on me that my first-born son will no longer be under our roof. He most likely will be spending his whole eighteenth year in treatment. Not with me, his mother. Not with our family. Not in our home. I got an overwhelmingly excruciating pain in my gut.

After taking a time-out with my head buried in the steering wheel, I decided I could not take the silence any longer. While blankly staring out the front windshield, I reached out and called Susan, my soul sister and best friend from childhood. During our young adult years, I was always by her side, supporting her as she struggled with addiction. Now it was her turn to hold me up. I was so grateful she answered the phone. The fact that she was on the other end gave me comfort. Susan was the only one in my life who utterly understood what my son was going through. She knew what to say. And she knew how to listen. When I hung up the phone, I unleashed buckets of tears. It felt cleansing. Then I called my parents. They are always there for me and now understand the breadth of what was going on with TJ. Talking to them helped me to compose myself. Eventually, I mustered the strength to enter the house, feeling so grateful for my pillars.

Later that evening

My heart felt tight in my chest as I prepared TJ's outfit for the plane ride he would be taking with his dad the next morning. I set the washed and folded clothes on a chair in the hallway outside his room to make things run as smoothly as possible when we woke him up. There wouldn't be any other luggage for the cross-country journey except for an iPad and earbuds to keep him from asking too many questions along the way. After saying goodnight with an extra-long hug, I closed his bedroom door. I paused there for a bit, my hand still on the knob and my forehead pressed to the door. I took a slow, deep breath.

The alarm is set for 4 a.m. Uber is scheduled for pick up. Tomorrow morning will be the last time I see TJ or talk to him for months. He will be headed to an off-grid location in Utah without wi-fi, electricity, or running water. Tonight, as he rests his head on a soft pillow, he is ignorant of the fact that the next time he tries to fall asleep, it will be inside a zero-degree sleeping bag on frozen ground with nothing but a tarp to protect him from the wind and snow. I can't believe it has come to this.

Intake Day

Friday, 2/23/18
I didn't get a wink of sleep last night. My stomach was tied up in knots. I tossed and turned and checked my phone to see what time it was, worried my alarm would not go off. My mind was busy thinking of how this was all going to turn out. What if TJ doesn't comply? What do we do then? There is no Plan B in place. It has to work.

When it was finally time to wake TJ up, Tom and I entered his room together to find him buried under a pile of blankets. I turned the lights on low and gently shook his shoulders until he was conscious enough for us to explain what was about to happen. His dad and I told him he would not be going to school. Instead, he will be traveling to Utah to help manage his depression. We thought playing hooky might rouse him.

TJ blinked as he tried to focus on us standing over him and turned his sleepy head back into the pillow. I peeled the blankets off and nudged him again. He didn't fall for the plan and the more we insisted, his responses became filled with anger and profanity. Using more authority in our voices, we told him he did not have a choice and asked him to be ready to leave the house to catch a plane. We left the room and closed the door for privacy.

Tom rubbed my back reassuringly as we impatiently stood in the hallway. I heard TJ swearing and then a punch to the wall. He may have reacted like this due to the hints of "rehab" that we would throw around when he continued to fail drug tests. His outburst was followed by a quiet, nail-biting waiting period. Way too much quiet time in there. Was he getting dressed? The Uber was outside, and we had a flight booked at 7:30 a.m. Anxiety welled up in me. At this point, I wondered if we should have listened to Teri's advice to hire a transport service.

Then suddenly, TJ's bedroom door creaked open, and he staggered out with unruly wavy hair and puffy eyes. He was angry, confused, and defiant-looking. But he was dressed. I felt relieved seeing him standing there in his jeans, t-shirt, and the vintage black leather jacket found at a flea market. But my relief soon changed to fear.

There was a hitch in the plan. TJ had a realization and began tugging at his hair in frustration. Compliance took an abrupt turn. "Oh, shit! ...I'm not going," he exclaimed. *What now?* With a hoarse and urgent voice, he told us how he loaned his vape pen to a friend the night before and refused to go anywhere without it. Ugh! Tom and I looked at each other with incredulousness, and I bit down on my lip. Putting a hand on TJ's shoulder, his dad desperately said he would stop somewhere on the way to the airport to find him a new vape. Somehow that did the trick. The early morning hours worked to our advantage because he surprisingly believed his dad on this one.

I walked toward the front door with TJ and showed him his shoes that were strategically placed in the entryway the night before. He remained silent. I was surprised he didn't wonder why he didn't need to pack his clothes. I handed him a bag of road snacks with a note tucked inside saying how much I would miss him.

Tango appeared from his bed to see what was going on. He stretched his front paws and leaned up against TJ's legs to beg for some attention. TJ bent down to hug his furry best friend and told him he would be back soon.

I embraced my not-so-little boy and whispered that I loved him in his ear. As TJ and his dad drove away on the cold, dark winter morning, sadness filled my heart. For some reason, I could not cry. I wanted to let my emotions out but only stood there with Tango, feeling frozen and looking blankly out at the lonely and empty tree-lined street.

Transport

Teri suggested we hire a youth intervention transport service to take TJ to wilderness. Families often hire transport services because they are afraid their child will act out or refuse to comply. The specialists who work for such transport teams are experienced in coordinating the details of safely escorting struggling kids to wilderness programs, residential treatment centers, and the like. Reputable companies know how to manage transportation in a compassionate manner and are trained to control and de-escalate situations. Many transport professionals have worked in other therapeutic settings such as wilderness field guiding, coaching, and counseling. Teens are usually awakened early in the morning by their parents or caregivers, who then introduce the transport team. When done properly, transportation becomes the first step of the therapeutic journey, by preparing the child for what lies ahead.

Tom and I thought it was too extreme to hire a transport company for TJ, who was not typically aggressive. Instead, TJ's dad accompanied him by plane all the way to the wilderness program. We figured TJ would not make a run for it because we had decided to leave out the details of where he was going and how long he would be away from home. Later, TJ would say he wished that we had used a transport team, believing it would have been more direct and less stressful knowing exactly what was happening from the start. Additionally, he mentioned to us that he missed out on sharing "gooning" stories with the other boys in his group. (Gooning is a slang word for transport, coined by wilderness students, and is a hot topic of discussion around the campsite.)

CHAPTER 3

REFUSAL OF THE CALL

The hero is summoned to the special world. *He is reluctant to leave the environment he is accustomed to at first. Perhaps he's afraid of the unknown. He refuses the call except he has no choice but to take on the challenge.*

TJ Narration:

Reflecting on the Events to His Mom,
One Year After the Wilderness Journey

Friday, 2/23/18

When you and Dad woke me up that morning, I was confused and hazy. I didn't have much sleep the night before, and I remember you handing me some clothes to change into, but it was still dark outside. Too early to get ready for school. You told me I was going to some type of "depression seminar." I knew something was up because you and Dad were acting strange the few days before. I broke into your computer to look at the history and saw you were searching for programs that I knew were for me. There was this big unknown. The bedroom door closed, and I was left by myself. I didn't want to go anywhere, I was so tired from being out all night, but I felt your presence outside my room. There were clothes waiting for me on my bed. I seriously considered jumping out the window and running away. Not sure where I would go, though, probably hide at Jimmy's house and then get caught.

I remembered I had loaned my vape pen to a friend the day before at school, and he didn't return it. When I told Dad I wouldn't leave without it, I was surprised he offered to buy me a new one on the way to the airport. I don't know why I ever believed him.

It then dawned on me to clear out some items in my room that you might find while I was gone. I rifled through my school backpack and jean pockets in the dirty hamper and found my vape juice bottles. I needed to dispose of the evidence. There were some pot brownies left over from my birthday. I took the stash out of my file cabinet next to my bed and ate the entire batch, which was about 400 mg. Your voices were murmuring through the closed door, and I felt pressured to change into my clothes.

The next thing I knew, I was at the airport with Dad. I was flyin' high, so I don't remember the exact details of the day in general. What I do recall is going to the bathroom at the airport, looking in the mirror and seeing my eyes were red as fuck. The Visine wasn't working. Worried Dad would notice, I tried to play it off that I was only tired. I slept most of the way anyhow, so I don't think it was noticeable.

After two flights, we ended up at this tiny airport, and by this time, all I knew was that I was going to some sort of camp. I figured Dad would rent a car and drop me off at a cabin. But this guy with a Jedi hairdo and a hippy-looking girl were standing there holding a sign that said: "TJ." I was so confused. I looked back at Dad, and he had tears in his eyes. It was the first time I ever saw him cry. His face was so sad. He said, "I'll see you later. I love you." I was thinking, "What the fuck is going on?"

Dad told the two strangers that I could keep my iPad to listen to music on the drive because it would keep me calm. Music has always helped me with tough times and made sense out of my emotions. It's an auditory reflection of what I feel inside. My body surged with anger as I held the iPad and left toward the parking lot to a big SUV with these people.

We first stopped at a medical clinic where I got a drug test and medical check-up. While sitting in the lobby, I asked the counselors, or whatever they were, some questions: "Where am I going, and who are you guys?" And "Why do I need to get a tetanus shot?" Jedi guy said, "Well, when you're out in the wilderness, you can get cut ..." Blah, blah, blah. I didn't listen to what he said after the word "wilderness." Then I continued with, "Well, okay, but aren't we going to be staying in cabins?" (Didn't Dad mention cabins?) I figured it would be for a week like all the other camps I'd been to. He said, "No, you will be going on backpacking expeditions in the wilderness."

I started freaking out more and more. I never liked hiking. "Uh, how long will this be?" Jedi hesitated, made a face that told me bad news is about to be broken and said, "The normal stay is about three months." (((FUCK))) That's when I totally lost it. My eyes got wide, the room felt like it was closing in on me, and I thought I was about to burst. Blood rushed into my face as this all hit me. Holy shit. I sat there in silence while I processed this information. I was speechless.

My mind was numb, and my body was boiling with emotion as I followed them out of the clinic and got back into the car. We went to this burrito place next, sort of like a nicer Baja Fresh. I'd lost my appetite by this time and needed to use the bathroom. Jedi guy followed me, and when I tried to close the restroom door, he put his foot in the doorjamb to keep it from closing all the way. I asked him what's going on, and he said, "I'm sorry, man ... I gotta do this." I didn't understand why I couldn't take a piss without him hovering over me.

Instead of relieving myself, I turned my back on the door, connected my iPad to the restaurant's wi-fi and started furiously texting you and dad. I regretted the things I said and still wondered why Dad let me have my iPad.

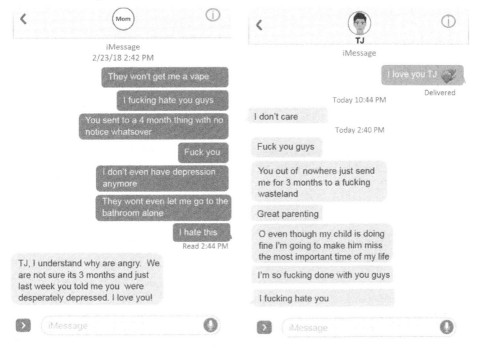

When I was done in the restroom, Jedi guy and I walked together from the bathroom to a table, and there's a burrito and drink waiting for me. I was so upset and refused to eat what was in front of me. That was a big mistake. What I didn't understand was that this was my last chance to have an actual meal. The two of them looked at me and gestured to the plate to encourage me to eat. I continued to sit there, blank-faced. Jedi says, "You're going to want this, man … trust me." Later I wished I had taken his advice.

Next stop, we went to this supply warehouse where I was sized and equipped for some heavy-duty outdoor clothing, boots, and other supplies. My head was still spinning, but then I was distracted for a bit by this little warehouse cat. The cat liked me or sensed how miserable I was and rubbed its side against my legs, purring. It was nice, but I was still numb-mad. Not showing any emotions on the outside.

When we returned to the car for the next leg of the trip, Jedi guy confiscated my iPad. I asked him why he took it, and he told me my parents sent screenshots of my previous communications to the higher officials, and therefore, I'd lost the only privilege I had left. Now I'd be without technology and my favorite music for months. I still couldn't believe they let me keep the iPad in the first place. I remained blank-faced.

We continued to drive, passing farms and small towns. My escorts tried to make light conversation. They seemed nice. When we stopped at a light in one of the towns, I took the opportunity to get the hell out of there. I started pulling hard on the door handle. It was locked. I attempted to unlock it, but of course, it was child-proof. No luck. So, I sat there quietly and looked out the window.

The rest of the ride seemed long and in the middle of nowhere. The weather was gray and cold, but it was warm inside the car. As we drove, it got darker and started snowing hard. The wind was blowing. I didn't see snow that often, so I got excited. I thought, "Oh, okay, we are going to be in the snow. Cool. I haven't seen snow in a while."

We made it past the first checkpoint. I could see the snow was getting really high. The car started to go off-road, and I was jolting and bouncing around in the backseat. The further we went, the more I knew I was fucked. I got a feeling this was not going to be comfort-able. We came to a final stop, exited the car, and started walking in the dark. I followed the guides up a gravel path, my boots making loud crunching sounds. I was wearing thick layers of brand-new hik-er clothes and felt like a stuffed potato. At that point, I was not mad anymore; I was defeated. It's like when a dog that gets shocked with a training collar rolls onto his back and says, "You win." Dropped in the middle of the desert where I can't buy weed. Checkmate.

It was now pitch-dark, but as we approached, I could see the glow of a fire through the snowstorm. Once we got to the fire, I saw peo-ple around it. They turned their heads to look at me. No one said anything. I was taken to a smaller fire pit away from the group. A staff member introduced himself to me, and then one of the boys broke off from the group, walked over to me, and told me he's my mentor. His name was Luke, and he had curly hair, these big glasses, and big eyes. I was told I couldn't talk to the other boys yet. I felt like I was tripping. All these emotions were being processed, and I kept thinking that I'm going to be here for three months. Someone offered me food in a tin cup, but I refused it because it seemed like hobo food.

When it was time to sleep, they showed me to a tent that had a sleeping bag on the ground. I tucked myself in the bag like a mummy. Someone took away my shoes. The guides slept on either side of me to keep me from going anywhere because I was on "run watch." I went to bed hungry, thinking of that burrito.

The next morning, I woke up in my tent and said to myself, "Where the fuck am I?" The side of my face was planted in the dirt because I slid off the mat in my sleeping bag. At first, all I could see were silhouettes of guys that looked like homeless people eating around a fire. Some were doing yoga poses in the snow. They were all curious, looking over at me, not saying anything. I thought I must have had a bad dream and still needed to wake up. But I wasn't dreaming. I was hungry, my breath was steaming, my cheeks were cold, and I could smell burnt wood in the air. Oh, and I had to take a pee. I decided to get up, fake it, and make the best of it. I didn't have any other choice.

CHAPTER 4

CROSSING THE THRESHOLD

The hero begins the quest by choosing to cross the threshold and transcends into the special world. This marks an official separation from chaotic home life and into the peaceful surroundings of nature. The parents and the child both begin their quest by committing to the journey and learning the lay of the new land.

Mom's Narration:

Parents Crossing the Threshold

In the aftermath of saying goodbye to TJ and Tom in the wee hours of the morning, I stood there in the open doorway, looking at the empty driveway and feeling shell-shocked. I lingered there for a bit and reflected on the day we'd brought our beloved firstborn child home from the hospital seventeen years before. My mother took a photo of us posing in front of that same crimson red door, gently cradling our tightly swaddled and ruddy-faced newborn. Tom and I were freshman parents in that picture, ready to give all our love and affection and oblivious to the many twists and turns to come.

Going forward, I decided that my hopes and expectations for my son would have to be put aside to make room for the present. It was there, at that same crimson door of my modest home in suburbia, that I now crossed the threshold into the *special world*. I referred to it as the dawn of my transformation from blind to sighted, unhealthy to healthy, dysregulated to regulated. One step at a time, I inched away from the spot where I gave my little boy one last hug before he left for the wilderness.

I headed toward the kitchen, where I made a pot of coffee. The sun was coming up, and a new set of challenges were about to begin. The house was so quiet I could have heard a pin drop. Tango went back to his favorite spot on the couch, and TJ's little sister, Beth, was still sleeping. I had a small window of time to regroup. Since I was homeschooling my daughter, I had the luxury of letting her sleep longer than usual before breaking the news about her brother's whereabouts. Armed with my cup of joe, I ventured into TJ's room.

Without him in there, it felt empty and bleak. I gazed at the walls covered with posters of rap music artists and surfers encapsulated in giant waves. The space that once was bedecked with Thomas the Tank Engine bedding and wooden train sets now resembled complete chaos.

His desktop, made from a plain wooden door, was scrawled with hand-drawn sharpie doodles of pop culture. There were clothes and trash strewn about, dresser drawers left open, and a dank, musty odor. I could smell weed. Using built-up nervous energy, I went to find the source by digging through shelves, and emptying pockets. There were vape juice pods, empty cartridges like the ones I found in the laundry. A fake urine bottle complete with a heating pack to nullify drug tests. Under the bed were more mysterious items. I scooped up shoes, duffel bags, something that might be a homemade plastic bong, a toilet paper roll stuffed with dryer sheets, crumpled notebook paper, and school hoodies. Everything was spilling into the hallway. Out went the empty "medical" marijuana containers and stripped-out highlighter pens for smoking who knows what. Gone were the clothes I would rather not see on him again. I purged and purged until the room was clear of remnants of his past world.

TJ's Acclimation to the Special World (aka The Wilderness)

Before launching on his eventful journey into the "woods," TJ needed to gain an understanding of why he'd landed in what he at first considered a wasteland. He spent the next several days acclimating to his unfamiliar environment. It was a period of introspection when he was most likely recovering from his exhausting day of travel and observing the new community. He was set aside from the rest of the group of which he was about to become an integral part. There he remained in solitude, near the warmth of the campfire. The assigned student mentor and field guides were the only people he spoke to during this time.

The foundation of TJ's outdoor program was modeled after the medicine wheel, an ancient and sacred symbol of health and healing used by the Indigenous peoples of the Americas for generations. The movement of the medicine wheel typically begins in the south and travels in the direction of the sun. Each element of the wheel is symbolic of the points of the compass (south, west, north, east), seasons of the year (summer, autumn, winter, spring), animals (coyote, bear, buffalo, eagle), aspects of life (emotional, physical, mental, spiritual), or elements of nature (water, earth, air, fire).

When the treatment staff considered TJ to be ready for the transition, he began his first round of therapy in the *Water Phase*.

The Medicine Wheel, Symbolizing Elements of Nature

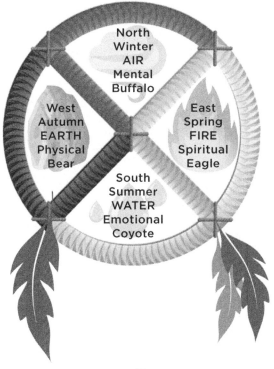

TJ's First Field Journal Entry:

Day Four in the Wilderness

Monday, 2/26/2018
Today I finally got to officially meet everyone on my team. After breakfast, I was sitting on my C-pack waiting to bridge when Jeff, the field guide, told us we were about to hold a ceremony. I was then blindfolded and guided up a steep hill. Once I reached the top of the hill, I was asked to take off my blindfold. I was on top of a mountain with all of Utah surrounding me in every direction.

Luke, my student mentor, introduced me to the medicine wheel. The team made a circle on the ground with rocks and gave me a ceremonial cleansing with sage incense. I was shown a lake in the distance and told all that it means to be in the *water phase*. This experience was unexpected and one I won't forget.

I feel like I've integrated into the team well and am excited to move on with my experience in the wilderness.

TJ 's Reflection on the First Journal Entry
Three Years After Wilderness:

I've been asked if I was still angry after my first wilderness ceremony, a valid question considering the optimistic tone of the journal entry. Looking back on this part of the journal is kind of a trip. At the time, I was still full of resentment and shock, but the journal entry seemed to appear optimistic. This was within the first few days of my time spent out in Utah, and at that time, it was the pinnacle of abhorrence to the situation I was in. When I first arrived in the group, I had been coming down off the weed I had taken before I left with my dad. I was shocked to have been stranded in the middle of nowhere in that manner. I felt like the plane I took to get to the "depression camp," or whatever the ruse was, had crash-landed and left me marooned with all these hobo-like hippies. So, yeah, I was pretty pissed off. Who wouldn't be? It seemed almost as if I had taken some drug like DMT and was transported into a whole different reality. In fact, I questioned if I had died or dosed something, especially in that first week.

Neurosis definitely played a role in my first week of optimism. There was no acceptance of the situation at that point. There was no talk of any aftercare plans and no set expectations of my future lifestyle requirements. From my recollection, other than the first 48 hours, the introduction week was somewhat fun.

My psychosis of being set on getting out of this situation was prematurely unshaken by my therapist Badger, so I still believed there was a way to manipulate my way out of the situation. Though I was resentful of my parents for sending me to the middle of the desert, I was still hopeful I could pull a prison situation of getting out with "good behavior."

There was no nervousness in meeting the other boys nor fear of being taken up the steep incline with a blindfold. Because I was such an egotistical asshole at that time, I wanted no part of that hippie bullshit, so I had subconsciously discarded the idea of making this situation work. I was determined to fake my way through the wilderness. What I didn't realize was that there's no real way of faking your way through that shit. It's easy to see when someone has a mask on. The wilderness sets up self-reflection, and though self-reflection is not the be-all cure, it is a start for change. The relationships I made with the boys were deep. I ended up knowing so much about them, I considered them brothers. It's hard to fake that.

Mom's Narration:

Parents Meet the Wilderness Therapist

Within a week of TJ's arrival at base camp, Tom and I were introduced to Jonathan Mitchell, a respected primary wilderness therapist. I felt like we had struck gold in securing our son a placement with Jonathan as his mentor. He is famously known as "Badger" to his mentees.

The word "mentor" originates from the ancient Greek epic poem *The Odyssey*. Mentor was the character whom King Odysseus entrusted to guide and teach his clueless and wayward son, Telemachus, while Odysseus left Ithaca to fight in the Trojan War. Just as Mentor guided Odysseus's child, Jonathan took the reins in mentoring our misdirected son.

On the initial call, we clung to Jonathan's words as he told us the account of TJ's first few miserable days. Jonathan sounded positive and inspiring and, at the same time, he didn't sugarcoat anything. He reported that TJ seemed "pretty bummed out" and kept to himself when he arrived. During an expedition, the windy conditions combined with detoxing from substances were the perfect storm for an almost uncontrollable anxiety attack. The guides walked him through the episode using emotional regulation skills.

Jonathan reassured us it was a good thing TJ was unraveling from the start, because it provided material for him to work with during their therapy sessions. He said the students who are compliant will hold their feelings in, check off the boxes, and not get deep into the therapy until late in the program. Our son had no problem laying it all out there, right from the beginning. It was difficult to hear how much he was struggling, but I was glad Jonathan had plenty of opportunities to crack TJ open to see what was going on inside him.

TJ met with Badger at base camp every week for individual and group therapy, so Badger could teach him the coping skills needed in this new and *special world*. By coordinating with the treatment team consisting of field guides, psychiatrists, and psychological test evaluators, Jonathan was able to make a recovery plan to suit our son's needs.

Self-Care

Grief and relief were two words that describe how I felt during the transition and adjustment to TJ being gone. My child, who I love more than anything, had consumed my life for the past few years with worrying, arguing, negotiating, snooping, and attending therapy appointments. I was wrung out and depleted of energy. There was a twinge of guilt in my stomach from enjoying the newfound peaceful household. I needed to process all these emotions, and it helped to turn my focus on self-care. The wilderness program stressed its importance.

With my best efforts, I worked on putting on my own oxygen mask before assisting others, as stated by all the articles I read about the subject. For me, this meant carving out time to write in my journal, taking yoga classes, getting to bed earlier, meeting friends for coffee, tending to my vegetable garden, and even doing nothing, without feeling remorse.

As I focused on self-care, it helped give me the energy I needed to write letters to my son and do the wilderness program assignments. TJ's dad did the same and even went further by exploring local meditation classes. Meditation was not something we had ever tried before.

In our letters to TJ, we wrote about specific things we were doing to make changes to our mental and physical health. We hoped it would give him the impression that we were not solely preoccupied with his progress and remove the pressure of being the only one needing to do the work. Tom and I also had the opportunity to attend a parent retreat hosted by the program, where we met other families whose kids were currently enrolled in the program with our son. During this workshop, we practiced yoga, meditation, and healthy communication skills and made self-care plans.

Therapeutic Assignments

Tom and I came to realize that once our son had gone to the program, we couldn't lie back, put our feet up, and expect him to succeed unless we took part in the work alongside him from a distance. We both had to dig deep into ourselves and examine deficiencies in our parenting skills. The program incorporated a family systems therapy approach, meaning they include parents, caregivers, and sometimes siblings by involving them in the healing process. We had assignments to do that were parallel to what TJ was learning in the field and followed along with the stages he was going through. There were recommended literature to read, webinars to watch, and podcasts to listen to. It was overwhelming, to say the least. But of course, it was not as difficult as what TJ was experiencing in the mountains. At least we were not sleeping under a tarp in the freezing weather. TJ had his own workbook consisting of mileage logs, goal plans, tips on how to survive and thrive in the woods, therapeutic exercises, and information on plants, animals, and constellations.

PHASE II: INITIATION

Once having traversed the threshold, the hero moves in a dream landscape of curiously fluid, ambiguous forms, where he must survive a succession of trials.

— Joseph Campbell, *The Hero with a Thousand Faces*

CHAPTER 5

SUPERNATURAL AIDS

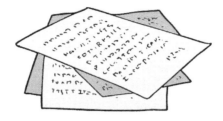

The call to adventure interrupts the hero's ordinary world. He needs magic helpers and tools to endure the journey. Below are some of the supernatural aids both he and his parents encounter to help them in the special world.

Letters

Letters written to and for particular friends: on the most important occasions. Directing not only the requisite style and forms to be observed in writing familiar letters; but how to think and act justly and prudently, in the common concerns of human life.

— Richardson, Samuel, *1689–1761*

Mom's Narration:

The only means for a sneak peek into TJ's mysterious new living situation was by way of a letter. Exchanging letters was one of the most essential and profound aids in the wilderness journey. As an empowering tool, it helped us reconnect with each other, lay the groundwork for more constructive communication, and thoughtfully set up boundaries. Writing also allowed us to take a pause and think before expressing what was on our minds, without reacting impulsively. Tom and I tapped away at our computers throughout each week, carefully crafting what we wanted to say. The act of writing letters was cathartic and emotionally exhausting, but I loved how it brought us closer to TJ the good old-fashioned way, minus the feather quill and inkpot!

Before receiving his first correspondence, we counted down the days and the hours as I bit my nails and paced the floor. Our feelings were a combination of fear, excitement, and curiosity. Was he keeping warm? Forming connections? Would he ever speak to us again? Weekly letters were exchanged through the outdoor program's online parent portal. Tom and I refreshed the computer all day long on the official letter-receiving day, hoping TJ had followed this writing assignment, or that he even wanted to connect with us. It turned out he did, and about three days into his stay, TJ's therapist scanned and uploaded scrawly and earth-smudged messages from him. They were accompanied by a handful of photos of TJ backpacking, hanging around the campfire, and brushing his teeth with a sullen-looking expression among snow-covered pine trees.

TJ's First Letters to the Family from the Wilderness

Letter to His Parents:

Monday, 2/26/18
Dear Mom and Dad,

My time here in the wilderness has so far been pretty peaceful, but I still can't get over your deception in getting me here. You guys said I would only be here for a small amount of time, but the average stay here is three months, and I can't help but feel totally lied to. You also said you would "take care" of my nicotine, but you didn't tell me I couldn't have it at all out here. I miss when I could lay in a bed and relax, then take a shit in an actual toilet and not in a bag.

Though I probably won't forget your lies, I miss you guys and Beth a lot. I wish you didn't send me away for so long for weed. I feel like you had it pretty good with me, from the stories I've heard around here. I also don't know what you're trying to accomplish with getting me off weed because when I get back, I'm not going to stop medicating myself for my back and neck pains which are excruciating out here, especially at night.

You say you understand what I'm going through, but now you really have no idea. The transition here has been hard. We only get to shower once a week, crap in bags and have to say our name over and over until we're done so they know if we try and run away, which doesn't make sense because where is there to go? I'm in the middle of fucking nowhere! Every night before I go to bed, I think of you guys, even though we only usually have surface-level talks.

I love you.
TJ

Letter to His Sister Beth:

Monday, 2/26/18
Dear Beth,

I wish I were back at home so I can see you and your quails. How are Lil Peep and the runt doing? I've been having a hard time at this camp; it feels like a long time since I've seen you already. I have realized how much you mean to me because I can see more clearly that you and I have a lot of the same troubles. I hope I get to see you when mom and dad come to Utah to check on my progress in a few weeks. When I get back, I want to take you out to get some frozen yogurt or to the mall, or whatever you want to do.

I hope I hear back from you soon.

Love,
TJ

First Letters to TJ from Home

Dad to TJ:

Saturday, 2/27/18
Dear TJ,

Since I got back from dropping you off, I can tell you that there has not been a waking hour that has gone by that I have not thought about you. I understand why you were angry, especially that you were not given any notice or information about where we were heading or what the program entailed. No one would like to be surprised in this manner, but it was necessary to get you there safely and start this journey.

I miss you terribly. I imagine that you may be missing some aspects of home—probably making music, your friends and possibly the comforts of civilization. I know that taking you away from those things is upsetting and feels unfair. But as we have seen over the past several years of struggling with the same problems in the same environment, we have not made any meaningful progress on how we interact, how you manage depression and particularly how you continue to self-medicate and participate in recreational drug use. Removing you from this environment at home is critical to allow you the time and space to focus on yourself and consider where these choices are leading you.

I want to make sure you know that I am hopeful. I feel confident that you will finish the program and that you will make choices that will lead you to a productive and happy life. And I know we can repair our relationships as there have always been glimmers of how positive it can be. Over the past week, I enjoyed spending time with you, for instance, troubleshooting the auto-tune ilok problem and shopping for the new skateboard.

I love you, TJ!
Dad

Mom to TJ:

Saturday, 2/27/18
Dear TJ,

I know that you feel a lot of anger right now. It hurt to read what you wrote in your texts on the way to the program, but I understand that you were acting out in pain. I thought of you all day while you were on the way to Utah. Signing you up for this program was not a quick and easy decision for Dad and me. We did this because we love you and were concerned that you were taking the wrong path by abusing substances to fix your depression and anxiety. Your choices have been putting a strain on our relationship for the past few years.

This is a chance to take the time to clear your head and turn your life in a better direction. You were not happy with school and living with us at home, which you expressed on many occasions. I hope you understand that this is not meant to be a punishment, but we did this out of our deep concern for your mental and physical health. I genuinely believe this experience will bring you closer to us and prepare you for your life ahead. Remember that this is only temporary.

I am going to miss you terribly while you are gone, and I am glad we will be staying in touch through letters. Dad and I will be doing some of the same assignments along with you and will be visiting you at the campsite when you are ready. The goal is to keep you healthy, safe, and close. You mean the world to us.

I love you so much, TJ.

Mom
XOXOXO

Mom's Narration:

Contents of the Letters

We wrote TJ two kinds of letters. First, there was the weekly correspondence, which was on the lightweight and newsy side. We would mention the latest antics of the family dog, Tango, or how our incubated quails laid their first eggs. Sprinkled throughout were photos of TJ's pets or lyrics from his favorite musical artists. For these interactions, we kept information about day-to-day family events to a minimum, not wanting to make him feel left out. To help him stay attuned to what he was experiencing in the field, we focused on reflecting on those things he had shared with us that he was doing or the emotions he was feeling from his previous letters. We incorporated the new communication tools we were learning, such as *I-feel* statements.

The other type of letters we wrote were the impact letters. They were more direct, and specifically written to help him understand why he was at wilderness and how his behavior impacted his world around him. TJ read them aloud to his wilderness group in a therapeutic setting, so his peers and the field guides could understand what he needed to work on and help him to process his feelings around them.

Throughout the program, the tone of TJ's messages to us went through various stages. In the beginning, he was rightfully confused and angry. There was a push-pull between him telling us how he did not need to be there versus us explaining to him why he needed to be there. Once he read the impact letters where we discussed difficult and specific incidents, he began to realize how serious we were about our desire for change, and he gained a deep grasp of how the only way out of his situation was to take it through to the end. It wasn't until then that he turned a corner and started relying on himself to make it to the finish line on his own instead of reaching for a life raft.

When our letters were ready to send to TJ, Tom and I emailed them first to the therapist for his review. This helped Jonathan gain a better understanding of the relationship we had with our son and allowed him to offer constructive feedback. Once approved, they were printed and delivered to TJ at base camp. TJ said it was a highlight of his day when word from home arrived each week, even though the messages were not always exactly what he wanted to read. His grandparents, uncle, sister, and cousin also sent him letters. TJ collected and stored them in his satchel to carry with him on expeditions and use as a reference as he corresponded to us in return.

Mentors

Primary Clinical Therapist

TJ's Narration:

I remember the first time I met Badger, my therapist. I was sitting with my team, resting on a log after being in the woods for almost a week. We had just returned from my first expedition. He comes walking up to the field, looking like the priest from *That '70s Show*. He had a full head of short wavy brown hair and a big toothy grin. On the outside, he seemed nice, so I let my guard down. But I found out that he's persistent like a honey badger. That's how he got his nickname.

Badger introduced himself to me before our group session. At the end of the meeting, he started taking the students one by one to have their individual talks. He walked with me up a trail toward this warm glowing fire and invited me to have a seat next to him in a camp chair. It was the first time I'd sat in a chair since I arrived. The heat from the fire felt soothing. He started asking me all these questions like, "What do you think brought you here?" He seemed genuinely interested in what I had to say, and it was the first time since I arrived that I felt connected to someone there.

The more I got to know Badger, the more I was convinced that he could read my mind. And none of the guys on my team could get away with lying to him, because he always seemed to know. You can't bullshit Badger. He always figured out if things didn't align together with what happened on the expeditions, to what we shared with him during our one-on-one time.

Mom's Narration:

Field Guides

Field guides are considered the backbone of Outdoor Behavioral Healthcare programs, which makes them important mentors. Their job is vital because not only do they safeguard the kids twenty-four hours a day, but they also teach students how to build their shelter, bust coals, cook meals, and stay hydrated and warm. As an integral part of the treatment team, they also manage therapy assignments, administer medications, plan ceremonies, teach mindfulness exercises, and help students process emotions right there in the moment.

The guides make it seem like living in the natural world is interesting and fun and not just a torture chamber where evil parents send their kids. While living alongside their mentees among the beautiful, rugged scenery, they learn what issues the students are grappling with, supplying them golden observations to provide the therapist after the expeditions.

Working with groups of kids suffering from emotional difficulties is an intense job. Hence, field staff are typically assigned alternating weeks to rest and recover between shifts. TJ became attached to certain guides and missed them when they rotated. Many guides choose this profession because on their time off, they can enjoy what they love best—outdoor adventures. When TJ graduated, he said he wanted to return someday to go on a camping trip with his favorite field instructor.

Peer Mentors

Another influential guide TJ encountered in woods was his peer mentor. When TJ first arrived, he was matched up with a wilderness student who had been there long enough to show TJ the ropes and welcome him to the community. The open enrollment structure of many outdoor therapy programs allows for student mentoring because new kids are continually entering, while others are exiting as they graduate; therefore, the group consists of students at all different experience levels. TJ's role eventually changed, and when he reached mentorship status himself, it gave him a sense of pride to be the one to look to for advice. This built up his confidence and became an important part of the growth process.

Bow Drill

Mom's Narration:

Making fire out of sticks using a bow drill is the heart and soul of Wilderness Therapy programs. It is an arduous process that builds discipline and teaches how not to give up. There are five basic parts to a bow drill: the bow, the bowstring, the rock socket, the drill, and the fireboard (see Figures on next page). The friction created by the fast-moving drill is what makes the coal needed to ignite the fire.

TJ's Narration:

Busting a Coal

Most of the guys in my group were used to saying, "Fuck it!" and doing whatever they want whenever there's a problem. So, when given this hard challenge of busting a coal, they needed to learn a no-fail mindset because they can't make it through the entire program without doing it. Failing is not an option. It's interesting to watch the new students in the group lose their cool when they are first starting out. I knew how they felt because I was so pissed off while everyone in the group watched me fail over and over. And it's not about strength. There was this football player in my group who couldn't make it happen as fast as he wanted. He got so discouraged because he thought by being big and strong, he should be able to do it right away. It's about focus, practice, and discipline.

Before learning how to bust a coal, we first had to make our own bow drill set, which was a whole skill in itself. On our hikes, we would search for the right quality and size tree branches to carve the pieces. Guides helped us by pointing out different sagebrush or Mormon tea branches they spotted on the trails and sawed them off for us. We put the "blank slates" (the raw wood sticks) in our backpacks and kept walking. At the end of the day, after setting up camp, we used whittling supplies to work on shaping and smoothing the wood. I spent a lot of time rounding out the spindle and carving a point at the end like a pencil. For the fireboard, I would form a 2x4 shape so it would stay steady on the ground. I drilled notches on the board and dug a trench for the punk to fall into. Making the bow drill set was an art form. Whoever had the best-looking kit in the group was admired. Our completed fire sets were like collectors' items. They were one of the best things out there for some of the guys.

The favorite reward for busting a coal was being able to eat a hot cheese quesadilla. We called them "cheesy tortes". They were cooked on flat stones in the campfire ring. After a long day of hiking and carrying our packs, there's nothing that tasted better. We were not allowed to eat them until we'd busted our first coal. It was hard for some of the guys not to eat the whole weeks' worth in one sitting. Everyone wanted to binge them, but we had to ration. The guides made a rule: one coal = one cheesy torte. That eventually had to change to one per day because the guys would keep making coals so they could eat a cheesy torte and then run out of their rations before the end of the week.

BUSTING A COAL   **BOW DRILL SET**

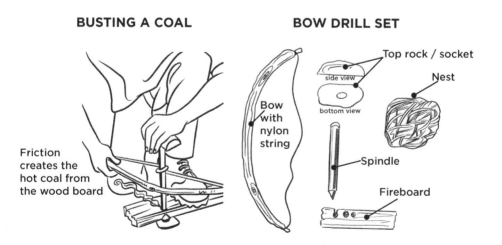

Communication

Mom's Narration:

I-feel Statements and Reflective Listening

Elements of effective communication language we practiced at the program were called *I-feel* and Reflective Listening. TJ implemented these tools with the staff and his teammates every day in the field, and it became second nature to him. When he needed to get something off his chest in an assertive way, he would say, "I'm going to bust an *I-feel*." Families at home were expected to practice applying *I-feel* statements in their letters, during their field visit, phone calls, at graduation, and beyond. This style of communication felt clumsy at first, but after some practice we could make it sound more natural.

The conversation works in two parts between speaker and listener. In the first part of the *I-feel*, the speaker tells their feelings in a constructive way while the listener truly listens. Then in the second part, Reflective Listening, the listener repeats what the person said, which results in the speaker feeling heard. It helps to clarify emotions without putting the listener on the defense and results in deescalating conflict.

Example of an *I-feel* Statement:

Chase: "TJ, I feel frustrated and angry because you didn't help clean the cooking pots. I feel this way because it was your turn. At this moment, I'm going to take a deep breath and stay calm. In the future, my request for you is to step up and do your share of the clean-up."

Example of Reflective Listening:

TJ: "Chase, I hear you say that you feel frustrated because I wasn't cleaning the pots and pans. I imagine you feel this way because it was my turn to clean. Right now, you are going to take a deep breath and stay calm. In the future, your request for me is that I clean up the pots when it's my turn. Did I miss anything?"

Chase: "I think you got it ... I feel heard."

I-feel Statement	Reflection
I feel (emotion word) when you (explain).	I hear you say you feel (repeat emotion word) when I (explain action).
I feel this way because I believe (describe belief).	You feel this way because you believe (describe belief).
In this moment, I am going to (describe an emotion regulation tool).	Right now, you are going to (an emotion regulation tool).
In the future, my request of you is to (action request).	In the future, your request of me is (repeat the request)
	Did I get that right? Do you feel heard?

Feelings Wheel

To help identify feelings, the Feelings Wheel tool came in handy. Once we recognized the primary emotion in the center of the wheel, we expanded to the outer circle to pinpoint a more in-depth and descriptive word. This incredibly helpful tool served as a feelings thesaurus. All I had to do was fill in the blanks in the *I-feel* statement, and voila! The mystery of labeling emotions is easily solved.

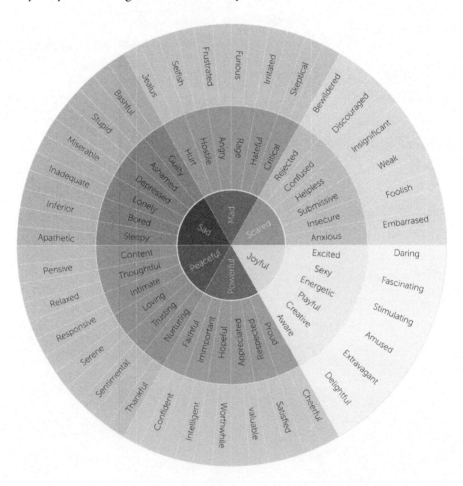

The Feeling Wheel was designed by Gloria Willcox (1982).

Validation

Validation is a powerful technique we practiced during the program to help us reconnect with our son and make sure he felt heard and understood. I found it to be a simple and straightforward way to strengthen our connection with him (and in all relationships, for that matter!) Validating includes listening, paying attention, nodding your head, showing empathy, and acknowledging feelings, without judgment.

To this day, I still must be cognizant of using my validation skills. When done effectively, it magically changes the tone of a conversation by instantly going from conflicted to connected. The amazing thing is, you do not even need to agree with what the person is saying, feeling, or doing to connect. We also learned that with validation it is not necessary—and often, it doesn't even help—to offer solutions or produce a similar story.

Examples of Validating My Son While at Wilderness:

Ineffective: (Emotion is not considered or the feeling is dismissed)
Mom: "I understand how you feel. It must be hard being away from home out there in the woods."
TJ: "No, you don't understand! You can't possibly know how I feel!"
Mom: "Don't feel bad about missing the prom. It's only one night. Mine wasn't that fun when I was in high school."
TJ: *Rolls his eyes*

Effective: (Focus is on the emotion instead of the content)
Mom: "I hear that you feel sad because you are missing being with your friends at home."
TJ: *Nods head*
Mom: "You are tired and frustrated with having to hike every day." (Then stop there.)
TJ: *Nods head, feels heard*
Mom: "You must feel proud of yourself for busting your first coal!"
TJ: *Feels satisfied*

As a mother, I so often find myself trying to fix everything. But what I found was that my son only wanted to be heard and understood.

Mindfulness

Mindfulness was a practice incorporated into the wilderness program for both families and students. We learned how important it was to focus on being fully in the present. Admittedly, living with an emotionally suffering, drug-using teenager had created a habit of parenting out of fear. I had to retrain myself to *respond* instead of *react*. This means taking the middle path, staying curious, asking questions, and not making assumptions. To help us stay present, TJ's dad and I practiced meditation, worked on deep breathing exercises, and employed feelings check-ins.

Breathing Exercises

The *Three-part breath* was a breathing tool to direct oxygen toward the lower belly, mid-chest, and upper chest. We would take three deep breaths in each section, filling our lungs to capacity before exhaling completely.

Feelings Check-in

SIFTing was a useful emotions check-in tool. We used this to recognize how we were feeling in the precise moment. The acronym stands for: Sensations, Images, Feelings, and Thoughts. It slows the brain down to gain awareness of what is going on with our body, mind, and soul. We wouldn't take a deep dive into these feelings, only a quick inventory before moving on with the day.

SIFT

Sensation: Short description of what you are feeling in your body.

Image: A visual impression of what is going on in your mind.

Feeling: Notice and name the feeling.

Thought: A simple description of what thought is passing through your mind at the moment.

Example: "My chest feels tight, my mind is doing backflips, I feel frustrated, I am craving ice cream."

CHAPTER 6

THE ROAD OF TRIALS

The hero travels over bumpy roads and undergoes a series of tests, tasks, and challenges, which are important to his growth on the journey. As he transitions to the Earth Phase, he looks for what is hidden beneath the surface and faces his emotional pain. He sits with his emotions and allows them to work their way through. There are miles of hiking, ways of learning to work with different personalities on his team, making fires for heat, and setting up proper shelter. Meanwhile, back at home, his mom and dad are working through their own set of trials.

Grief

Mom's Narration:

The Five Stages of Grief

While separated from our son and processing his being away in the wilderness, we experienced what is called the stages of grief. This concept was originally developed by Elisabeth Kübler-Ross to apply to grieving a death, but it can relate to grieving any kind of loss, whether it be the loss of a relationship, the loss of a job, or the loss of your child's normal trajectory. It had never been part of our hopes and dreams for TJ to leave our family for months during a momentous time in his life to live in the boonies of Utah. While he was at the program, the disruption seemed so monumental that it was hard to see past it. Simultaneously, TJ was going through his own cycle of grief out in the woods. His letters and journals reflected shock and anger about his situation. He was living in unfamiliar territory and was homesick.

Examples of Mom's Grief:

Denial: In the beginning, when the situation at home with TJ was on a downhill spiral, I wanted to believe his behavior was normal teen angst. We chalked up the drug use to teen experimentation. When we were told about Wilderness Therapy programs, I thought this was too extreme of a treatment for my son, who does not even like to hike or go to summer camp. Once he was there and friends asked where he was, I stretched the truth and told them he was on an extended camping trip.

Anger: I blamed the kids he hung around with, his ex-girlfriend, social media, legalization of marijuana, and the world we live in. I was jealous seeing Facebook posts of my son's friends posing in their tuxedos and formal dresses before school dances, smiling and looking happy. Or seeing photos of their school sports, college visits, and family trips. I felt sorry for myself when I saw kids in the neighborhood walking or riding their bikes to school. I was frustrated at hearing nonstop talk of SATs, college apps, or moms complaining about their trivial (in my opinion) child-rearing problems when my son was missing an important time of his adolescence to live in the wilderness and an aftercare program. There was a time when I disclosed where TJ was to a friend whose children were on "normal" paths. She responded by saying, "Oh, it will be okay when he's done. Don't worry. I know someone else who had a comparable situation with their kid, and he turned out fine." My blood boiled! How could she know it would be fine? She would never know or understand!

Bargaining: Upon hearing the recommendation that TJ transition from wilderness to aftercare at a therapeutic boarding school for nine to twelve months, I tried to convince myself he would do fine if he returned home and saw his therapists regularly.

Depression: I stayed composed for the world around me until something like a song would set me off, and then the tears would come rolling. My first-born child was missing an important part of his life, and I was not going to physically be with him. I was devastated. I felt lonely because no one around me understood what I was going through. I came to the realization that I was done mothering him at home, because he would be turning eighteen soon. It was too early to let my baby bird leave the nest.

Acceptance: I stopped trying to compare my son's life progress with that of everyone else's child and realized that they all have their own journeys with their own struggles. Friends in my inner circle noticed how calm and resolute I had become from the new mindfulness skills I had learned. I felt grateful for taking the journey because it changed me as a person in a positive way. Important life lessons and enlightenment would not have occurred if my son had not taken this detour.

Examples of TJ's Grief:

Denial: (Quote from TJ's letter)
I wish you didn't send me away for so long for weed. I feel like you had it pretty good with me, from the stories I've heard around here.

Anger: (Excerpt from TJ's journal)
I realize I feel the most depressed I have felt in a while. I feel totally disconnected from the world and everyone in it. I miss my mom so much, to the point that I would do anything to hear her voice over the phone. I hate Wilderness Therapy and everything it has to offer. I wish my dreams were less vivid; all of them have been so crazy. They are making me feel worse and worse. Last night I had a dream that I was in a hotel hallway and saw my mom pass by me. I tried to reach out to her, but she didn't recognize me. I've been trying all day to decipher what this dream means. So far, I have not had much progress. This has made me angry about being in this shithole! I am so FUCKING ANGRY ABOUT EVERYTHING! FUCK THIS SHIT! FUCK BOW DRILLING! FUCK THE DESERT! FUCK BADGER! I can't even call my parents! This is so stupid! I miss everything at home. My FUCKING parents sent me here just because I don't want to conform to their FUCKING SHIT! FUUUUUUUUUUUCK!!!!!!!

Bargaining: (TJ's letter)
Dear Mom and Dad, being in the wilderness made me have a psychotic breakdown. Every day I have to carry a 70 lb. pack on my back, which is torture because of my back pain. Though there are moments of fun, it doesn't outweigh the suckiness of the

three-hour hikes, doing the exact same thing every day and the high chance of getting sick. I don't know why you thought this was necessary to fix our relationship. You guys never really tried hard to talk to me in-depth. Most of my memories of us are only first-level conversations, and you are punishing me for weed. I want to have a relationship with you, but the way you go about it is super weird and extreme. I think if you sat me down, talked to me for a while, and treated me like an equal, we would have a better relationship. I'm seventeen now, and in a year, I'm going to be able to legally smoke weed, so I don't know why it's such a big deal to you. A couple of days ago, I felt like I was on an alien planet and couldn't get off. This place is suffocating me. Doing the same thing over and over is awful. I feel like I'm living in Groundhog Day. It's literally like this ... wake up, eat breakfast, pack up, hike to a new spot, dinner, and sleep. Over and over. I barely have time for myself. I feel like I'm always being watched, which is a terrible feeling. I think you could handle this situation better, instead of spending 500 bucks a day to send me to this literal shithole. We are actually sleeping next to cow shit at the moment. There must be something else you can do. I really want to talk to you on the phone. Please try to make them let us have a phone call. I feel like I'm in prison because I'm not allowed to even talk to you over the phone. I miss you even though I'm angry. Love, TJ

Depression (TJ's letter)

Dear Dad, I'm sad and disappointed that we haven't been closer over the past few years. I feel like I know nothing about you, and that makes me bummed because it seems like all my friends know a lot about their dads. Maybe it's this way because you are so invested in your work or spending time getting me better that you don't focus on yourself. Whatever the reason is, it makes me sad that I feel like I barely know you after seventeen years of being with you. Most of the people here are going to aftercare for around a year after this place, and that makes me worried. What is your plan for me, and when will I get to come back home again? I realize now how much I like being at home and going to school. I would like to come home and see how everything has changed and hang out with you. Maybe if I finish in time, I can come with you to the Grand Canyon. I hope you can open up to me and we can get to know each other better. Love, TJ

Acceptance (Excerpt from TJ's journal)
Walking through the valley, my feet and back hurt from carrying my C-pack on my back. I was feeling disconnected emotionally and spiritually from this land, like I'm marching through a foreign place on the way to fight another tribe. I sit, take a sip of water, and close my eyes to take me away for a moment. Suddenly, I hear a screeching sound, so I take a peek at what's making a ruckus. I see a figure soaring through the sky, swiftly, like a knife cutting through butter. A hawk and its partner were playing in the air, dogfighting as if they were two planes in battle. Their dance was magical, like two ballerinas on the dance floor. Enchanted by their showmanship, I looked around at the scenery, realizing how bright all the colors were around me. The trees were dancing along with the two hawks; the nature in Utah seems to be all connected. I feel like I'm at peace and content with this land.

Weather

Mom's Narration:

Tom and I worried obsessively about TJ living in the elements during winter and checked the weather day and night. We didn't know the exact location of base camp but set our cell phone weather apps to the general area. When we found out storms were coming in, guilt would wash over us as we lay our heads down on soft pillows at night and pulled the covers to our chins. Curiously, TJ never complained about the weather in his letters. The guides and staff taught him how to take care of himself, and he was equipped with proper clothing and gear. He slept in a negative-20-degree sleeping bag. It turns out that we did not need to worry about the weather because Mother Nature's wrath is a necessary part of the journey. TJ got wet but learned to stay dry. He got cold but learned how to stay warm. The storms came, and the storms went. And miraculously, he persevered.

TJ Narration:

Ups and Downs from the Field

Waterfall in the Shelter

One night, I set up my tent on the side of a sheer wall of this mountain after we arrived at camp in the middle of the night. Because I was so tired from the long hike, I didn't tie the knots for my shelter securely. The weather was relatively calm earlier that day, so I figured it would be okay. Later while I was sleeping, I felt water dripping down on my face. At first, I thought I was dreaming, but then it started sheeting down, which woke me from a deep sleep. I had to take down the entire tent and reset it at the bottom of the hill in my underwear and socks while the wind was blowing, and it was pouring rain. I was always careful after that to set up my shelter properly and tie my knots securely.

The Quinoa Story

We had to stop and set up camp earlier than usual one afternoon because of a crazy lightning storm that came over us. It happened to be in this place with the most beautiful view of all the mountains. Everything was surreal to me because not only were the colors in the sky vivid from the lighting, but I was also feeling out of whack from coming off weed and antidepressant medication. This goofy kid in my group named Chad was cooking that night. He took the cooking oil and dumped most of the bottle all over the quinoa. No one could eat the final product because it tasted like burnt gelatin. We were not allowed to waste any rations, though, so the guides kept passing it around and made us finish ALL of it. I had the feeling of being in an altered state during this time. Eating terrible tasting oily quinoa and laughing like a madman. I lost it. I threw the quinoa on the ground and yelled, "I'm NOT eating this fucking quinoa!" I must have seemed like a lunatic as I couldn't stop laughing while the thunder and lightning were going off. All my emotions were coming out. Since leaving the wilderness, I've vowed to never eat quinoa ever again.

Letters Between TJ and His Sister Beth:

TJ to Beth:

Monday, 3/12/18
Dear Beth,

I just woke up in a shelter I built out of a tarp and rope on top of a mountain overlooking all of Utah for about fifty to one hundred miles. This week has been hard, but I'm going to be telling you about all the cool things that happened.

When people here are ready emotionally and physically for a transition point in their stay, we hold a ceremony for them that is accompanied by a challenge. My friend Evan was ready for one, so his ceremony consisted of him digging a six-foot-deep hole in the ground and him being "buried" in it. We put sticks over the hole. This was representing the old Evan being dead and us putting him in his grave. It seemed like he sat there for hours, contemplating his old life and his future.

Yesterday, Evan, one of the guides, and I decided to go on an adventure, so we left the team behind and looked for ancient civilizations. We found things that the guides, who know the lay of the land, have never discovered. There was an ancient well that was still full of water in the middle of the desert. We found three primitive houses built into the top of a canyon wall and a mill where they stored and ground their grains. That was one of the craziest things I've seen in a while.

It's time for us to get up for the day now, so I've got to go. I hope to hear from you soon.

I love you,
TJ

Beth to TJ:

Friday, 3/16/18
Dear TJ,

How's it going? It seems strange without you here. I saw pictures of you in the desert. It's so awesome that you found an ancient village. How many times do you get to shower, because it looks like you rolled in dirt? I heard you made cinnamon rolls in the campfire. Were they made from scratch?

I really hope you get help for drugs and depression so I can have my brother back. It made me sad when I came home, and you and your friends were high, and I could smell weed from your room. I also don't like talking to you when you have been smoking weed. I miss you, but I'm glad you're there getting help.

Well, I've got to go now.

Love,
Beth

TJ to Beth:

Thursday, 3/22/18
Dear Beth,

It's hard to live out here, especially because I have a sore throat right now. I'm around the same people every day, and I'm getting tired of it. Yesterday, I moved to the next level in the program, so I'm a step closer to coming home. I want to apologize for all the stress I've put you through in the past. I feel bad I wasn't a better role model for you. When I get back, things will change. I'll be getting a car and will drive you around wherever you want to go.

I love you and miss you.

Love,
TJ

TJ's Field Journal:
Friday, 3/23/18

Bow drilling has been a struggle for me. Not only because I can't get a coal, but also because I want to make my mom proud by making her a fire at the family visit. I feel upset and unaccomplished because I feel like other people can get coals with ease, while I have trouble even getting smoke. I know if I persevere and keep a good mindset, I'll eventually get good at it, but it's hard because I keep getting into my head about it. Yesterday, I finally made a big step. I prepared my set well, and I finally got a coal on firewood, which is a hard thing to do. This boosted my confidence a lot, and now I feel much more motivated to continue bow drilling. Hopefully, by the time my parents get here, I'll be a confident bow driller, but all I can do for now is to continue to try hard and persevere to be the best I can be.

Letter from TJ to Mom:

Saturday, 3/24/18
Dear Mom,

This week has been emotionally stressful for me because I realized a lot about my time before coming here. I thought a lot about my work here and realized that a lot of what I do is for you, not me. I want you to be proud of me. In the past, when you expected me to keep my grades up, play sports, and be the person you wanted me to be, it made me sad. I also want you to understand me. I was frustrated when you didn't agree that weed was positively affecting my creativity and helped my self-confidence. I resented you and was angry.

My guides pulled me aside today from the team and asked me to find three things my eye was drawn to. I found a pinecone, a crystallized rock, and a stick of a Mormon Tea tree branch ... all of which I found esthetically pleasing. They told me to meet them on top of Eagle Rock Mountain and asked me why I chose these items. I said I thought my mom would like them. They told me that it seems like I dedicate all my work to my mom and to think of how I can dedicate my work to myself. I was then told to meditate on top of the mountain overlooking the west canyon. After this time, I transitioned to Earth Phase. It was an eye-opening experience. I earned my backpack. I'll tell you more later if you want. I love you. TJ

Mom's Narration:

Neuropsychological Testing and Medication Evaluation

Field Visit from a Neuropsychologist

When TJ was a few weeks into the program, his therapist and EC strongly recommended he undergo a neuropsychological evaluation to help provide an additional layer of assessment. Before Tom and I understood the importance of having this test done, we felt like we'd been knocked sideways. For one, the expense was additional to the already hefty price tag of outdoor therapy. We thought the testing TJ had already done through his school district for his IEP was sufficient, but it turned out the prior evaluations were outdated and not comprehensive enough. More importantly, we were told that psych tests are required by most aftercare programs prior to acceptance.

Once we understood the reasoning behind the request for a full evaluation, we swallowed the price tag and decided to go forward with it. Our EC referred us to a neuropsychologist who travels all over the country to evaluate students onsite at various wilderness camps. He met with our son at base camp in a quiet, climate-controlled portable room where he administered written and oral assessments. TJ said he didn't mind being plucked away from his group because the room was warm and was a nice break from the elements. The advantage of undergoing the testing in wilderness was the fact that TJ had been free of substances for a month at that point as well as removed from the distractions of the world, which made the test results more accurate.

The battery of tests included IQ, cognitive functioning, ADHD, areas of strengths and weaknesses, academics, learning disabilities, underlying emotional functioning, capacity for distress tolerance, personality patterns, and much more. The final extensive and thorough eighteen-page report was incredibly helpful to the treatment team and aided the EC in making appropriate aftercare recommendations. The majority of the cost ended up being covered by insurance, and we were grateful to have this incredibly useful road map of our child's brain.

Field Visit from a Psychiatrist

Finding the right prescription medications for TJ's mood disorders had always been a challenge. They did not work well, and he never liked the way they made him feel. A psychiatrist who had been contracted by the program met with TJ in the field to create a new plan. He contemplated either making an adjustment to the current medications or discontinuing them altogether. While coordinating with his doctor and therapist, it was decided to try weaning TJ off all of them while he was in the wilderness. We were relieved that TJ was under tight supervision while detoxing, in case he experienced uncomfortable withdrawal symptoms. When he had changed medications in the past, he experienced manic side effects and had suicidal ideation. The outdoor therapy program was a safer place than home in which to do this experimenting.

CHAPTER 7

APPROACH TO THE INMOST CAVE

After becoming familiar with the special world *and making it through the initial road bumps, the hero approaches the inmost cave. This stage is described as a dark and scary place where the treasure of emotional resilience resides. By getting to know his dragons, he heals and frees space to expand and deepen his understanding of himself. Reading the impact letters and talking to his parents via satellite is a turning point for him. The hero begins to gain more of an understanding of why he is there and realizes that no one will rescue him from the situation but himself.*

Impact Letters

Mom's Narration:

The impact letters were a way to tell our son, "We love you, and this is why we signed you up for Wilderness Therapy." Such a letter is designed to have an impact, as its name implies, by describing how serious we were about him changing the way he coped with his emotions and how his behaviors negatively affected those around him. Most importantly, the impact letters helped him look at his past behavior and provided a jump-start on the deeper emotional work ahead.

Students take turns reading their impact letters aloud to the group and field staff, who, in turn, support and give constructive feedback. An interesting dynamic is that the universal reaction to fellow students' letters is that their peers' digressions were far more egregious than their own. Before TJ received the most difficult correspondence from us on this journey, he was in denial that he needed treatment, based on his judgement of the other the boys who had already read their impact letters. This led TJ to believe that we as parents had it easy with him and should let him come home.

TJ's dad and I began composing drafts of the impact letters within the first few days of his departure. It was emotionally draining for us to revisit memories that were painful. We wanted to make sure to emphasize how much we loved him and what we loved about him, to counteract the more difficult elements of the letters. Badger inspected our first drafts and provided valuable input. We took his advice and rewrote. And rewrote again. The impact letters were the most pivotal messages TJ would be receiving, and they had to be just right.

I was paralyzed with fear thinking of TJ reading the impact letters we wrote that would confront him with everything on our minds. After we sent them, it took an agonizingly long time to confirm they'd been received. The guides waited for the right moment. When it was time, TJ was presented with the letters so he could read the colorful version of his backstory, as penned by us, his parents. After reading them, he could not deny that they revealed unhealthy patterns in his past, which were what had gotten him there in the first place. With this moment, he began the work from the bottom up.

Family Call

TJ Narration:

Finally, I had a phone that was connected to my parents from a place so far away. I had overwhelming emotions knowing they were on the other end. Their voices felt like strangers yet gave me comfort. I was next to Badger in the front seat of his truck with the heater on. It felt strange being in a car after a month in total wilderness. Sitting in a car, talking on a phone. I recall looking out the front windshield and seeing an outline of trees through the sunset as we spoke. It made me cry.

Mom's Notes from the Family Call:

Monday, 3/26/18

Tom and I were nervous to talk to TJ for the first time since he had left. All day long before the call, we were worried about what to say to our own son. The call started before TJ got on, so that Badger could give us a general recap.

Badger told us TJ was making good strides and was the "emotional leader for the week" because the advanced guys in the group were having a tough time. They were going into their dark holes, so TJ had needed to step up. He said TJ was nervous to talk to us. Badger then brought him into the call.

The conversation was at first slow and awkward, with short answers. TJ then began describing his experience at the program. At the beginning of his stay, he said, he was having vivid dreams due to the detox and didn't know if he was awake or asleep. The land looked like another planet, which made him feel disconnected from the world.

When he first arrived, he said he didn't do his own emotional work, that he had talked about other people's experiences and spent his energy learning the hard skills. This past week, something had changed in him. It all started when he was using the bow drill to bust a coal, and it wasn't working. He said he got angry, feeling emotional and sad. Then he realized the anger was because he felt like we don't understand the reasons he used substances. It made him emotionally distant from us. He felt like we should have talked to him more to understand that he used weed to numb himself and mask his emotions. He didn't know of any other way to make himself better. He felt upset that we thought he was becoming an addict.

TJ said when he read our impact letters to the group, he cried from reading about all the things we love about him even though he had let us down. At this point in the call, he broke out into sobs. Badger took over and suggested taking a break to allow TJ time to regain his composure. Right then and there, they both went through some deep breathing exercises together.

When TJ calmed down, he felt ready to explain some of the things he had learned about himself, his friendships, and his family while there. Tom and I focused on our listening skills and validated his feelings. We used the *I-feel* statements we had been practicing.

Before the call was over, we told TJ how much we loved him and that we couldn't wait to spend time with him on our family visit. After the call, we collapsed from emotional exhaustion.

TJ's Response to Mom's Impact Letter:

Tuesday, 3/27/18
Dear Mom,

I want to start this letter off by apologizing for all the stress I've caused in the family. Your letter got to me, not so much because of the things I've done, but because you expressed how much you still love me. It seems like you had done everything you could think of to get me better before you sent me off to wilderness. I feel grateful you put so much effort into keeping me safe and also happy. It seems like you were between a rock and a hard place and were worried about my safety and future. I heard you couldn't get close to me because of my interest in drugs, and that makes me sad because of a choice I made. You couldn't talk and be real with me. I also take accountability for not being more open with you and Dad. I wasn't receptive to your feedback, and I hope to work on that in the future.

At the beginning of my depression, some days, it was life or death to be kept away from my thoughts, so I used substances like alcohol to keep me calm. Neither therapy nor your support was helping my depression, and my destructive relationship with my girlfriend was making things even worse. I needed an escape. You and Dad had a hard time watching me in such an unstable place. I'm grateful that you kept me safe when I was contemplating suicide.

Regarding my weed use, I'm sorry my behavior got so out of hand. Since being in the wilderness, I've reflected on my relationships with friends and realized they were ruled by the substances. I feel embarrassed and ashamed that I brought substances into our home and allowed pictures of me on social media abusing drugs.

Ashton has gotten out of control with his drug use, and I don't want to be associated with him anymore.

Labor Day was a tough time for me and must have been for you. I was upset because I felt powerless, and even though what I did was disrespectful, I felt angry about the situation with Dad and how that made me feel. The morning I stormed out and ran away was because I wanted to feel self-reliant. I felt like you and Dad saw me as a stupid kid, so I wanted to prove to myself that I could live without your help.

I felt terrible that I wasn't a better role model for Beth and for the stress I put her through. I wish I hadn't been so obvious as to let her see me taking paraphernalia items from around her playhouse. I wish she was oblivious to the fact that I got high so I wouldn't have scared her. You seem sad and disappointed that your little girl was exposed to my lifestyle choice at such a young age. I hope to make it up by driving her places in the future and being a caring brother. I realize how my actions negatively affected Beth and her anxiety. I love and care about her so much.

Because of your hard comedown on substances and requirements that I play a sport and keep up my grades, I felt as if I had to conform to your rules without question and do what you wanted me to. I felt angry, sad, and trapped, so I decided to use the only coping skill that I knew worked well ... smoking weed. I didn't care about your rules because of how disconnected I felt from you when I was high. I know you only wanted the best for me and felt cornered because nothing you were doing was working. I think a big part of the disconnect was a lack of communication and lack of trust, which left me feeling that I couldn't be vulnerable with you guys. Hopefully, in the future, we can try to open up more and validate each other's emotions more so we can both be heard.

Halloween night was a scary time for me. I regret drinking so much, and after that night, I stopped drinking excessively. I can't say that I will never drink or smoke again, but I want to let you know that I realize the extent of how my actions affected you in the past, and I want to change my attitude and how I view both you and Dad.

A lot of my actions were pushed by your rules and reactions toward me. I felt disconnected from the family, so my friends made up for that connection I was craving. It was difficult for me to talk to you about my weed use because I was so worried I would be punished. This pattern will continue if you don't respect or support me if I continue to use drugs after I turn eighteen. It hurts me to know that someone who is supposed to be there for me won't be because of a decision I make. I understand your strong disapproval toward substances, but I feel disconnected when you won't even see my reason for using them.

I miss all the times I've felt close and connected to you, and I hope we can have more chances in the future. I want to find a way to spend the summer at home with you, but I understand why you would be so concerned with me coming home. When I read your letter aloud to the group, it made me sad to hear all the good qualities you see in me after how disrespectful I've been in the past. I started sobbing in front of my team during that part. I hope I can spend some time at home eventually because I'm homesick, but I want to let you know that I'm taking full advantage of my opportunities here. I've had a lot of realizations and changes in myself over the past few weeks. I feel like a ball of clay drastically being shaped.

I love you and miss you so much.

Love,
TJ

TJ's Response to Dad's Impact Letter:

Wednesday, 3/28/18
Dear Dad,

I miss the times we would go to Mammoth and ski. Also, it makes me sad that you don't see me as sweet and compassionate anymore. You probably stopped seeing that in me when I started being in my own world and feeling policed all the time. My teenage years have been hard managing depression and anxiety, and it has been especially hard to manage your rules. I felt like a criminal at home because of the choices I made. I couldn't talk to you, which must have been hard for you because you wanted to understand me so badly.

It seems like you have tried everything you could think of to help me with my depression. Now I know you and Mom really care about me, and that's why you gave me consequences. Most of the time I am with you, I feel trapped because you will do anything it takes for me to be who you want me to be, and that has put a great amount of pressure on me. Weed was something I used to feel free from you guys, so the punishments made me want to use more. I feel sad that our relationship has been destroyed by my use of the substance, and I hope we can repair things.

I realize that weed has made you concerned about my health and well-being. Though it has played a negative role in our relationship, I still feel like cannabis has aided me in a lot of my life, such as my interest in schoolwork and self-confidence. I do understand your point of view about how it has put my health and my development in danger. You must have been concerned that I would go down a bad path, thus felt the need to stop me from using it. In the moment, it was hard to talk about that with you because I had tremendous anxiety that you would punish me and see me as a bad person.

I feel bad about the way I treated Mom in the past. A big reason I would get so mad is that I would feel sad and frustrated about not feeling heard. I can imagine you must have felt sad that a lot of our relationship was bickering because that's how I feel too. I feel ashamed and sad that I called you and Mom names because I love you and don't want it to be that way. I hope to avoid this negative communication in the future by advocating for myself and using coping skills. I also want to be more mindful when I'm getting upset.

Rap has been a big part of my life for the past few years. I'm sorry about the way I portrayed myself by playing it at inappropriate times, which made you upset and offended the family. Though you told me to turn down my music, I never understood why it upset you because I view the lyrics only as words. A big reason I used outrageous lyrics in the songs that I wrote was because I got good reactions out of them. I had lots of people tell me they liked it, so I felt justified in doing it. I realize now though people may have liked it, it was disrespectful and not how you raised me.

I've taken the time to think about a lot of my relationships and realized many of them have been toxic or unhealthy. I still value my relationships with them, and I'm sorry that I fit in with these people.

I want to let you know I'm using my time at wilderness wisely and learning a lot about myself. I hope we can have a better relationship in the future.

Love,
TJ

Mom's Narration:

Aftercare Decisions

Wilderness Therapy is a stabilization period. Aftercare is the rehabilitation, or glue, phase—with the goal to make it all stick. When TJ was more than halfway through the wilderness program, the task of planning aftercare was front and center. Everything had been thrown at Tom and me during this time. My head was spinning from all the different choices there were. We were keenly listening to the advice from Badger and Teri, our educational consultant. Both recommended residential treatment. We also were absorbing messages from TJ, who was begging to come home. I read scary online reviews of abusive programs. At the same time, I read about success stories from online support groups. Mixed up in the middle of this confusion was my motherly instinct telling me to bring my child home. It was hard to see through the smoke and the noise produced by so many important and far-reaching choices. But Tom and I knew one thing for certain: we did not want to risk throwing away all the amazing growth and maturity TJ had so far accomplished in his wilderness program. Now that we were on such a good track, we did not want to make a mistake that might negatively affect the rest of TJ's life.

We were grateful for Teri, who was continuing her job as chief executive of operations to heal TJ. She was slowly gaining a better understanding of him through the weekly Badger calls and reports, reading TJ's letters, and studying his psych evaluation results. Teri collected and put together the critical information she needed to help Tom and me make the best possible decision for TJ's next step. She zeroed in on several programs chosen out of thousands available across the country. By making calls to directors and staff, she inquired if spaces were open at appropriate schools during the time TJ was projected to graduate from wilderness. She also regularly investigated on-site clinical therapists and sought to know what kind of students were currently enrolled in these particular programs.

Teri presented three aftercare options she felt were appropriate for TJ. The next step was for Tom and me to do our own research on these chosen programs. I pulled myself away from letter-writing and therapy assignments to speak with parent referrals and arrange travel to visit the schools in person. It was a stressful and time-consuming project.

I came to realize that there are a multitude of residential programs available that specialize in different kinds of issues. But first, I examined the two main categories: residential treatment centers (RTC) and therapeutic boarding schools (TBS). I discovered there's somewhat of a gray zone between the two. RTCs are known to be focused on the behavioral and emotional aspects, with academics of secondary importance, whereas TBSs usually have therapy secondary to academics. Confusingly, this is not always the case because the labeling of aftercare as "RTC" or "TBS" also depends on the licensing requirements of each individual state.

Besides learning about the differences between the classifications of programs, there are other aspects to consider, such as how tight or loose the "containers," or facilities, should be. Some places are lock-down centers, and others are secured only by staff. Some programs are in rural areas and include equine therapy and outdoor activities, while others are in suburban neighborhoods where students are integrated into society on a more regular basis. Other things to compare are how visitations, therapy, and communications are handled. When would TJ be able to earn his phone back? Was he allowed to have music, computers, and social media? How did they arrange home visits? Did they use a level system? How are academics handled? What is the therapist-to-student ratio and staff-to-student ratio? How involved are the families in the therapy?

Even though our choices were narrowed down to three core programs, we were still confused and stressed about selecting the best course of action for TJ. A few factors came into play in our decision-making. We knew TJ would thrive in a place where he had more freedom to live and work in society. In fact, we wanted him to practice living in a realistic environment where he could be in a safe bubble yet have room to take steps backward and be supported by professional staff who knew how to handle relapse. Another essential element we were looking for was our ability to visit TJ anytime we wanted. The program we zoned in on was an all-boys TBS in Utah that had no restrictions on visitation and was more like a home within a beautiful suburban neighborhood. There was a schoolroom on the premises where he could finish high school at his own pace. It also included extracurricular activities we knew TJ would enjoy, such as skateboarding, snowboarding, and wakeboarding. Additionally, the boys were taken on monthly out-of-town trips.

Teri suggested that we be open-minded and not choose a program only because it had pastimes TJ enjoyed. But I'll have to admit, I didn't listen to her advice on that one. Knowing my son, I could not picture him spending a year on a ranch doing equine therapy. In hindsight, I think it could have also been a positive experience for him to do something outside of the box.

When we had a clearer picture of what TJ's next journey might look like, all we had to do was sell him on the plan. Thankfully, Badger was already preparing him for the next stage. What was on our side at that point was that TJ was still under eighteen years of age and didn't have too much say in the matter. Nonetheless, we did want his cooperation and buy-in.

CHAPTER 8

ORDEAL

After facing his personal dragons and coming to terms with them, the hero discovers an enlightened version of himself. This stage symbolizes a death and rebirth. He is about to be pushed to the edge, becoming vulnerable and stripped from his old coping mechanisms. The deeply personal work ahead includes solos and fire vigils. Once the hero is reborn, he will be able to begin the long journey toward home.

Solos

TJ's Narration:

I had two solos where I learned to be with myself in silence to reflect on myself with no other distractions. The first one was when the whole group broke out and did solos at the same time in different areas of the camp. For the second one, I was the only person in my group doing the solo. It lasted for one night and two days.

During my solos, I busted fires and kept them going. I prepared and cooked my own food, meditated, wrote in my journal, threw rocks, organized sticks and leaves, and drew pictures in the dirt. There were moments where I became frustrated and bored, but I mostly liked it because it gave me time alone and away from the group. It's hard to put into words what I went through emotionally, but it helped me grow and learn about myself. It definitely changed me as a person in a good way.

The Solo

Nearly every mystic, saint, or prophet in ancient times was born from time alone in the wilderness. Solos is a time to be with oneself. It is a time to tolerate, and eventually appreciate, our own company, which is the first step toward realizing our own greatness.

— Jonathan S. Mitchell, MA, LPC

TJ's Field Journal (On Solo):
Thursday, 3/29/18

My eyes are crusty, and my head aches. I've been sitting in the same spot for about a day now, thinking a lot about my past and my future. I'm sad things turned out the way they did. Now I'm stuck in the desert. The only way out is working through this fucking program. Though I love my teammates and guides, I am sick of being here and would do anything to hear some music right now. The only thing I've heard for the past day has been either silence or the wind blowing back and forth. The wind is so irritating. It keeps blowing ash from my fire pan onto me and all my stuff. It's difficult being alone with my thoughts. I'm forced to think about everything. I would do anything to change things.

TJ's Field Journal (Fire Vigil):
Saturday, 3/31/18

Last night my team and I had a group fire vigil. We started by hiking eight miles to a campsite called Big Rock. Because we hiked so many miles and had to climb down a long way into the rocky campsite below, we abandoned our packs for the night and lived from the land, drinking water out of seeps. We had to make a fire from the materials available to us. To ask the land for permission to be with her, we cut off strands of our hair and buried them as an offering. Since doing this, I've felt like I am now a part of the earth rather than inhabiting it. Chris, Chad, and I went to collect wood for the night's fire. While we were collecting wood, I talked to Chris about how I've been feeling about possibly going to aftercare. I realize now that I've been suppressing my feelings about it and feel sad that I might not get to see my friends for a long time.

These last few moments I've had in the desert have been worthwhile. I feel peaceful with the earth, though I'm exhausted from no sleep. The fire vigil started right when the sun came down, and we stayed awake all night tending to it. The way this vigil was planned was to pay tribute to the medicine wheel. The moon: time for play, creativity, and learning. We started out telling stories we made up. Some of the new guys opened up to us about their lives because everyone was opening up. We laughed, listened, and connected on a surface level. This round loosened me up to what was to come. The second round was *Earth Phase*: emotional exploration ...

TJ's Letter to a Friend from Home:

Thursday, 4/5/18
Dear Jimmy,

You're probably wondering what the hell happened to me disappearing suddenly. I heard my parents told you a little bit about where I am and what I'm doing, but they don't even know the full extent of what this place is. Lately, I've been doing well at a wilderness program that takes you through each stage of life in a matter of about three months. I've changed a lot mentally since you have seen me.

Right now, I'm in the Earth Phase, *which is where there is a lot of emotional exploration. I've been mentoring new students now because I founded a new team, "Eagle," which will have kids come in and out of it for a long time. I've been working hard to move to the "Air Phase," which is leadership, so I've been reflecting a lot by doing a fire vigil. A fire vigil is basically staying up all night and tending the campfire, which is like a vision quest. I'm currently in the middle of my fire vigil. It's late at night, and I've been watching the stars, which are amazing out here.*

Recently, despite doing well and progressing in the program, I've realized that I've been suppressing my grief over my old life. At the beginning of my stay, I recognized that my habits back at home distracted me from my real emotions, gave me tunnel vision, and blinded me to the point that a lot of what we were doing was unhealthy and dangerous. I constantly drift my mind to wondering if you and people back at home are okay and safe because we could have really fucked ourselves over at times. Is everyone okay? Though I'm not going to be around, I want everyone to be safe because I value and cherish the times we all had together and hope I can be back in time for college to see you again. It's tough because I'm in Utah, and I'm probably going to be at a residential treatment center after this place, and I miss my old life at home. I hope to hear from you soon and hope you can update me as much as possible.

Miss you,
TJ

Being Stuck
by TJ

Peering through my telescope, I see
A pair of eyes looking back at me
A porcupine stuck in a tree
He walks, talks, and looks like me
Locked in a room inside his house
He slips out just like a mouse
Contemplates life on the couch
He wonders what it's all about
I don't think he understands
There's nowhere else to turn
Because time keeps wasting
Time is like a leaf in the wind
You're covered by the spikes
And trapped in your own sins
And you're left pacing
Don't waste it

(Written while on solo)

CHAPTER 9

ATONEMENT

The previous steps up until now have been preparing the hero for a chance to make amends with the family. Atonement helps lift and free the hero from places where he was emotionally hung up so he can move on to the next stage of the journey.

"I didn't understand the meaning of nostalgia until now."

— TJ

Family Field Visit

Mom's Narration:

About halfway through the program, Tom and I traveled to base camp to visit TJ, where we were able to observe in person how far he had come. It was not exactly a lightweight camping trip where we roasted marshmallows and told ghost stories. There was heavy emotional work cut out for us. We reconnected and practiced our new communication skills with the guidance of a specialized family therapist. During this intense and pivotal time with our son, we were rewarded with a greater understanding of one another and a return of the closeness that had gone missing somewhere along the way.

In Wilderness Therapy, field visits are not typically planned ahead of time, because the primary therapist needs to assess when the students and families are ready to put their skills to the test. Tom and I needed to be prepared to clear our schedules last-minute. Once Badger gave us the green light, we booked airline tickets and a four-wheel drive for the journey to base camp within a week.

Before our three day camping trip with TJ, Tom and I had a phone session with a therapist named Adam who was assigned to work with us. We discussed the background details about TJ and our family so he could put together a treatment plan and set goals for our time together.

Field visits are distinctive for each family according to their different dynamics, issues that need to be addressed, and sheer logistics. Some may occur a few days before the wilderness graduation, while others are mid-stay. The weather can also affect the experience. Fortunately for us, we didn't have to brave a blizzard or rainstorm.

Mom's Journal:

One Day After Flying Home from the Field Visit and Touring RTCs

Saturday, 4/14/2018

Tom and I arrived home from visiting TJ at base camp and a side trip to tour prospective therapeutic boarding schools. When I opened my duffel bag to do the laundry, a pungent smell of sage and campfire burst into the room. I had to step outside to shake out the silty Utah soil that had stowed away with my belongings. Smoky aroma clung to every fiber of my clothes, and it took my heart and soul straight back to the place where we'd had a magical experience as a family. I decided to leave my scarf unwashed, as a token of remembrance.

While the washer was running, I sifted through the pile of mementoes that fell to the floor. There was something in there I wanted more than anything. It was a cloudy and beaten-up plastic sandwich bag containing my souvenirs. I snapped apart the zip-lock to retrieve what was inside and carefully placed each item on a decorative tray on my dressing table. There was a "nest" made of shredded juniper bark for kindling, a carved wooden spoon, a rust-colored heart-shaped stone, and a white sage bundle. Before we said goodbye to each other in the *special world,* TJ had wrapped the sage with twine for me to take home as a parting gift.

One Day Before Our Family Field Visit

Sunday, 4/8/2018

It felt nice to leave home and breathe in the Utah mountain air. Tom and I spent our first night at a hotel in a charming Old West town. This trip was a much-needed getaway where we explored the shops and had some time to review the therapeutic homework assignments over dinner at a quaint BBQ restaurant before heading up the mountain to be with TJ.

Family Visit Notes: Hopes and Fears

- *I hope we can have fun, laugh together, and reconnect with TJ*
- *I hope I express emotions clearly and let TJ have his feelings heard*
- *I hope TJ respects our boundaries*
- *I fear he will be depressed and angry about our decision to transition him to aftercare*
- *I fear he will shut down on communication*

Base Camp Arrival

Monday, 4/9/2018

We woke up early the first morning to prepare for our drive to base camp. Knowing we would be seeing TJ for the first time in *forty-eight days* gave me goosebumps. We packed the car with one lightweight duffel bag to share between us for two nights of camping and a rolling suitcase put aside in the trunk for the second leg of the trip to tour therapeutic boarding schools. Aftercare was something we planned to discuss with TJ during the family visit. Although he was already aware that coming home after wilderness might not be a possibility, the thought about dropping the news on him in person weighed heavily on my mind. Fortunately, it would not be a complete shocker because Badger had already been planting the seeds.

We left the hotel to meet our family therapy team. They gave us the address of a coffee shop in a small town below base camp. The drive was about thirty miles through scenic mountain passes and beautiful farmland. Tom and I were amused that our first destination was a vintage gas station-turned-microbrewery among the cattle ranches. It was graced with a gravel parking lot surrounded by diesel pickups and Suburbans. Congregating customers were a mixture of overall-clad, leather-skinned ranchers together with granola-loving transplants appearing to be pursuing a less plugged-in rural life. Additionally, we noticed a hive of other Wilderness Therapy families and guides coming through. This mom-and-pop café was a modern-day silver mine.

As we stood in line to order lattes, the barista looked at us knowingly and said with a gruff voice, "You're early. What can I get you?" She nailed us at first glance as city-slicker parents there to meet the wilderness guides.

While we sat outside anxiously waiting with drinks in hand, a white SUV turned into the lot. We assumed the two ruggedly dressed people emerging from the vehicle were the wilderness staff we were looking for. Sure enough, they introduced themselves as Adam, the therapist, and Rachel, the field guide. Adam looked like Johnny Appleseed with an earflap hat and a plaid flannel shirt. Rachel was a vision of Gaia, the Greek Earth Goddess. She wore a crown of mahogany braids around her head and a colorful wool shawl. We acquainted ourselves and walked outside to a small crimson-red bridge overlooking a gently running stream. It was a peaceful setting where we were led through a few stretches, deep breathing exercises, and a discussion of our hopes and intentions for the quest.

We took turns doing a feelings check-in. Mine sounded something like this:

My shoulders are tense, I see a bridge, my heart is happy, I'm feeling anxious.

We drove behind Adam and Rachel for a few hours on dusty unpaved roads through the desert toward base camp. Except for a few scattered farmhouses and dilapidated barns, there weren't many signs of civilization. The road started to climb toward the mountains until we eventually turned into a discreet dirt parking lot. As we gathered our belongings from the trunk of the car, Adam collected our cell phones, watches, and jewelry. He also took our medications and would be the one to administer them to us as needed. Tom and I would be without possessions, without time, without electricity, and one with nature. Just like how TJ had been living for the past six weeks.

Adam and Rachel escorted us to a footpath that curved through scattered scrubby pinyon pines and sagebrush. This was when I sensed TJ's presence all around me, yet the first glimpse of life was of an adolescent girls' group. They were trudging along the trail, returning to camp from an expedition, looking like a herd of pack mules. Their giant backpacks were swinging with Nalgene bottles, metal pots, and cups, making clinking sounds, sharply contrasting with the eerie silence of the desert.

It felt so surreal, almost like observing animals at the zoo. We all looked at each other with curiosity. Their families, I imagined, were at home thinking about them at that moment. Seeing real wilderness kids in action doing what TJ had been doing for the past six weeks had me feeling elated. Before this moment, I could only guess from TJ's letters and pictures what that scenario would look like.

We stopped at a rudimentary pump that supplied the base camp with water. The girls had gathered around to fill up their Nalgene bottles and then plopped onto a log nearby to rest. Rachel began pumping water into big white plastic containers for our three-day supply. Tom jumped up to help. When he noticed there was soil at the bottom of the containers, he asked Rachel if they should rinse them first. The girls overheard him and chuckled in amusement. Realizing he had an audience who looked as though they had survived an apocalypse, Tom sheepishly went about filling the containers ... with the dirt remaining at the bottom.

After the girls were done resting, they stood, said goodbye to us, and disappeared beyond the path. Brushing shoulders with these strong young girls had me wondering again where TJ was. Adam had disappeared a while before, and I felt like Rachel was keeping us in suspense. Tom and I stayed at that spot on the hill and waited for Rachel to direct us where to go next.

Leading us through a few deep breaths as we waited, Rachel crept closer to us and carefully removed each of our sunglasses. We were asked to close our eyes. I felt Rachel's hands resting on my shoulders as she slowly and gently turned me around, then Tom. With my eyes closed, I felt like I was moving in slow motion. I blinked them open and squinted in the bright sunlight. Twenty feet away was a lanky boy holding a walking stick, standing there and looking straight at us.

There he was. TJ was wearing a slightly crooked bucket hat and a giant backpack rising above his head. When he smiled at us from ear to ear, my heart fell right through my hiking boots, and my eyes were instantly brimming with tears. He leaned sideways to remove his backpack and started running toward us, with his arms spread wide. I couldn't reach him fast enough to hug him. All three of us wrapped our arms around each other in a triple hug. Tears were now rolling down our faces.

TJ smelled like a mixture of sage, BO, and campfire. He said he had just showered and used sage as an underarm deodorant so he would smell good and look clean for us. There was something he wanted to show me. Still sniffling, he looked down and gingerly took out of his pocket a pretty rust and silver-colored pebble. He had found it on the trail and been saving it for me for this day. I thanked him and embraced him again, not letting go, telling him how much I loved him. TJ said being hugged felt good. Hugging or physical contact of any kind between students and program staff is prohibited, and he missed being embraced.

With our spirits lifted, we started to assemble our things to carry to the campsite. There was a little awkwardness being together again in this new situation with so much to say but not sure how to say what was on our minds. TJ broke the ice by challenging us to pick up his backpack. I made the first attempt, but it was so heavy I could barely lift it off the ground! It seemed unimaginable to hike for miles every day, carrying a leaded beast on my back under the desert sun. Tom took his turn raising the backpack, grunting with exertion as he handed it back to TJ. With extraordinarily little effort, TJ proudly slung it onto his shoulders.

Rachel reappeared, rolling up with a wheelbarrow loaded with firewood, food supplies, and sleeping bags. We continued up the trail, which led us to a camping area where we would be isolated—together—for the next few days. TJ had set up a tarp shelter before we arrived. We tossed our duffels underneath the tent and felt ready to enjoy special family time.

Opening Ceremony

TJ and Adam prepared a medicine wheel for an opening ceremony, using sticks and rocks to form a large circle on the ground. They divided it into four quadrants to represent the stages of life. We were asked to search the area for objects to represent positive and negative energy. I found a heart-shaped jade-green stone to signify love and renewal, a piece of animal bone to embody strength, and a ragged piece of p-cord string to represent broken connections. We took turns explaining our chosen symbolic items before tossing them into their prospective locations. Next, we performed a smudging ceremony and turned our backs toward the wheel. With a bundle of smoldering sage, TJ rolled the aromatic smoke from our heads to our toes as he performed a chant that sounded something like this:

Smudge your head to open your mind for positive thoughts.
Smudge your eyes to see the truth.
Smudge your mouth so that you speak in an honest and kind way.
Smudge your heart to cleanse any resentment and open it to compassion.
Smudge your arms to carry your load.
Smudge your legs to walk you through.

Busting a Coal

This is the moment we had all been waiting for—witnessing TJ making a fire with a bow drill set. Excited like a little kid at Christmas, TJ pulled out the bow from his backpack. He asked me to help him collect shredded bark from a nearby juniper tree to make a "nest" for kindling.

Moving into position with his knee resting on a mat, he began pushing and pulling the bow back and forth. It was slow and deliberate at first, then gradually sped up, creating a clattery sound when the pieces of wood rubbed against each other. We were excited when we saw smoke rising from the end of the spindle. But then he lost control, and it flung into the air. Muttering profanity under his breath, he failed at several more attempts. In a matter of moments, his pride was swept away, and the mood changed to gloomy.

Tom, Adam, and I felt his pain. I wanted to help him but knew it was impossible. All I could do was stay positive and hold back from feeling completely enmeshed in his emotions. This bow drill exercise seemed perfectly built to prevent family from jumping in to rescue or fix. How many parents can help their kids make fire with sticks?

Furrowing his sweaty brow, TJ took a break and sat next to me on a log to simmer down. I rubbed his back in reassurance.

Still feeling deflated but determined to try again later, TJ agreed to tandem coal with Adam to get some heat going, as it was starting to cool off with the sun sinking. "Tandeming," as he called it, means two people handle the fire set by moving the bow drill back and forth in unison. As they worked together as a team with the bow drill, I could smell the smoke from the friction of the spindle on the fireboard as soon as they successfully busted the coal.

Gently tapping the smoldering black coal dust into the nest, TJ blew on it slowly, and it burst into a bright yellow fire. He placed the flaming nest into a fire ring using leather fire gloves. We collected sticks and logs to feed the blaze, and an inferno of bright heat cracked and twisted toward the sky. It gave the air an intoxicating burnt-pine aroma that amazingly seemed to melt away any tensions we'd been feeling.

Reconnecting

The sun began to slide lower on the horizon, casting long shadows on the desert floor. I scooted by chair back because, as our campfire gained strength, it was frying my face, and the ash was blowing in my eyes. Rachel handed us cozy flannel blankets to wrap around our shoulders.

This peaceful outdoor setting provided us with a fresh, clean slate. I wanted to focus on being in the moment and not think of our upcoming therapy assignments. Peeling my eyes from the roaring fire, I turned my gaze toward my son. He had this new "wilder" look, reminiscent of a boy right out of *Lord of the Flies*. There was a patch of scruffy whiskers sprouting from his chin, overgrown locks covering his ears, and lines of dirt caked under his fingernails. The grueling hikes had made his tall frame even leaner than it was before he left home. Despite looking rough-and-tumble, underneath there was a kid excited to share with us his accomplishments in the wilderness and happy we were there to watch and listen. His eyes and teeth seemed brighter, and I figured it must be from the clean diet of raw oats, fresh fruit, and veggies.

TJ went on to explain where he was on his journey. He said he was close to advancing to the *Air Phase*, a leadership level yielding more respect and privileges. What he looked forward to most was earning a coveted headlamp.

The highest level was the *Fire Phase*, and he aspired to achieve this status before he graduated, although it was not a requirement. Doing so would give him the privilege of "knowing the future," where he would be involved with planning and mapping hikes with the guides. When he mentioned he wanted to be a role model for the incoming students, I wondered if this was the same kid we had said goodbye to six weeks earlier. Tom and I hadn't seen this kind of motivation in him for a long time.

As we ate a delicious and healthy meal of veggie and cheese quesadillas prepared for us by Rachel, TJ talked about things he missed so far away from civilized society. Chocolate, hamburgers, and rap music were among the few. He was curious about what was going on in the world and wondered if there were many messages stored up on his phone. Did his friends know where he had disappeared to?

These questions and more he asked as he carefully whittled a tree branch into the shape of a spoon, explaining that when he first arrived at camp, he had to eat with his fingers or a stick until he carved his own spoon.

As the sun was nearly setting, we cleaned up the campsite and prepared to settle in after a long and emotional day. The three of us lined up our negative-20-degree sleeping bags, and like sardines, we snuggled under the star-draped sky.

I thought we might chat a bit more, but TJ fell asleep as soon as his head touched the ground. Although I was disappointed, after I thought about it for a moment, I knew that was probably for the best because we had a big day ahead. I couldn't fall asleep right away but listened to him breathe in the quiet of the night and felt content.

The Therapeutic Work

Tuesday, 4/10/2018

Family therapy was sandwiched between exploring the desert, eating healthy camp-cooked food, and listening to Rachel strum beautiful songs on the guitar around the fireside. Our discussions brought out all ranges of emotions, from warm and fuzzy to feelings of discomfort. The uncomfortable parts turned out to be the ones we learned and grew from the most. TJ, Adam, Tom, and I sat in a circle between pine and juniper trees for our group sessions with prepared notes at hand. Adam led the topics and knew when to jump in to help us out or stay on the sidelines. Rachel chimed in at times with meaningful and constructive comments when she was not hauling wood for our fire or preparing meals.

We worked on *I-feel* statements and reflective listening, which had become a second language for TJ. He showed a sense of pride as he smoothly verbalized his thoughts. I found it sweet when he politely guided us through our mechanical and unpolished statements to make sure we did them correctly. Mine started out sounding a bit awkward, but eventually I was able to work out my feelings. When one of us did an *I-feel*, the receiver would then exercise reflective listening by repeating what the speaker said to make sure they felt heard and understood.

What surprised me the most during therapy sessions was how TJ's dad, the person who never cries, became a waterworks. On the other hand, my tears were bottled up. I wondered why this was. Perhaps it was because I was thinking too hard about what I was saying and how I was saying it, instead of letting go and feeling. When all eyes were on me during my time in the circle, I became a deer in the headlights. This frustrated me because I wanted the emotion to match the *I-feel* statement. Looking over at Tom, I would see the tears rolling down his face. TJ was taken aback at witnessing so much emotion coming from his dad.

One of the subjects we needed to broach was aftercare, which had been the elephant in the woods since we arrived at the camp. The word "aftercare" meant TJ would not be coming home to his family, his friends, his room, and his school to finish his senior year. Adam helped TJ process the news of our decision to enroll him in a therapeutic boarding school. We tried to explain how the progress he had made would likely be upended if he returned to the exact same environment at home. However disappointed TJ was upon hearing this, he surprisingly held it together better than we could have imagined. He had figured out by now this was probably going to be what was coming next, because most of the boys in his group went on to aftercare. What helped soften the blow was that he already knew about one of the programs we were considering. Some of the boys on his team told him about it at camp and cast it in a favorable light.

The 4-Rs Assignment: Resentments, Regrets, Respects, Requests

Throughout our stay, we worked together with Adam on the "4-Rs" assignment: *Resentments* (hurt and anger we carried from the past), *Regrets* (things we did or said that we felt remorse about), *Respects* (qualities we admired in one another), and *Requests* (what we ask for in the future to help strengthen our relationship).

A critical item was cracked wide open during this assignment. The topic was *Resentment*, and it was about a particularly upsetting confrontation between TJ and his dad. TJ was caught blatantly smoking weed in the house after he had promised he would quit. This ordeal happened on a school night while we were at the dinner table with his little sister. We heard explicit rap music blaring and smelled the skunky odor of cannabis coming from down the hallway. Tom was at his wits' end because TJ had broken the rules right under our noses again, and this resulted in Tom unleashing his anger with some harsh words. Although TJ regretted destroying our trust, he was deeply hurt by his dad's response, which prompted him to run away.

While in our group session, Tom expressed regrets about the way he had handled the incident. The two of them had different interpretations of what had gone down and couldn't see eye-to-eye. The hurt feelings and resentment remained unresolved at this point. Tom felt that his relationship with his son was at stake. When Adam realized that the discussion was going nowhere, he called a time out.

Suggesting we take a hike to lighten the mood, Adam led us on a trail toward a bluff overlooking the desert with a view of the Four Corners in the distance. We climbed down some steep boulders to explore an ancient grain storage turret built by Ancestral Puebloans. Although it was interesting and fun, it didn't keep TJ from emotionally distancing himself from us. With his head hanging down, he asked to be left alone and sat with his feet dangling over a boulder. He told us he "felt small," looking out at the endless Utah desert.

On the walk back to camp, TJ said he was frustrated at not being in control of his life. He also decided he didn't care anymore about moving to the *Fire Phase*. My heart sank. All the good feelings we'd shared at the beginning of the trip had disappeared, and I wanted to somehow fix everything but didn't know how. I felt helpless, and it terrified me to see him depressed. When we tried to continue with our 4-Rs assignment back at camp, TJ choked up and started sobbing uncontrollably. We were not sure where to go from there.

Bow Drilling Saves the Day

Excusing himself from the group session, TJ wiped his tears on his sleeve and went over to his backpack to take out his bow drill. He'd decided he was going to bust a coal. Without saying a word, he patted the sweat off his forehead and bent down into position. We sat there motionless as we watched him push and pull the drill back and forth, with strength and determination. The look in his eyes said he was not going to give up this time.

After numerous tries, the smell of burning wood filled the air. Adam presented TJ with the leather fire glove like a gift on a golden platter. TJ held the smoldering nest in the glove so he wouldn't burn his hand, gently blew on it, and, like magic, it ignited in flames. The act of busting a coal instantly shifted the energy all around us, and it was nothing short of a miracle! Through the brightness of the orange and yellow blaze cradled in his glove, making an orb of light, I could see confidence beaming in TJ's face. The moment was priceless.

TJ was eager to teach his dad and me to tandem with him. We spent the rest of the afternoon busting fires. It was a great distraction from our difficult therapy session and pretty much saved the day by breaking the communication barrier. TJ and his dad's teamwork helped to build a sense of closeness between them. We were able to resume the therapy in a better frame of mind, and TJ and Tom resolved their differences. They validated each other's feelings and agreed to disagree on some things. Father and son atoned.

That evening we had the pleasure of meeting Badger in person. He stopped by the camp after the group therapy with the team and joined us around the campfire under the stars. We gave him a recap of how our visit was going, and TJ expressed his feelings around learning the news about going to aftercare. We were hoping he would commit to sobriety after spending so much time being clean, but he said he could not imagine himself living a life without substances. Badger stressed that three months in the wilderness would not be long enough to instill lifetime changes and that TJ still had a lot of emotional work to do.

Atonement

Wednesday, 4/11/2018

Parting with TJ the next day was such sweet sorrow. The hugs were long-lasting, and our hearts were open wide. Throughout our time at camp, we made big strides in our relationship and could see how much TJ had already grown. Before we left him behind in the woods, we gave him our good pen for letter and journal writing and a sunscreen stick that smelled like the beach. They were valuable treasures for him to squirrel away in his backpack. In turn, TJ gave me a bundle of sage he had collected and carefully woven together with twine, to remind me of our time spent together. Then he rifled through his pockets and pulled out a smooth and solid wooden spoon, the one he had been carving for the past few days. Gazing at his dad with love in his eyes, he placed it in the palm of his father's hand and closed his fingers around it. An olive branch.

There was no time or place to shower before our long drive straight to the airport. It was unfortunate because we hadn't changed our clothes for three days and the campfire/body odor puffed all around us as we sat in our seats on the puddle jumper plane departing for Denver. I felt terribly sorry for the passengers in our vicinity.

The plane jolted and started whirring as it was getting ready for take-off. I looked out the window at the mountains and thought about TJ being out there somewhere. He was not with us, and the motion of the plane speeding into the sky, far away from TJ, brought out a flood of emotions in me. A dam broke, and I lost control. My whole body was shaking with sobs. I turned my face to the window and covered my head with my scarf. Tom rubbed my back, and that made me cry even harder. I couldn't stop if I tried.

Built-up tears from the past few days and the past few years came flooding out. I was crying for the situation we were in, crying because I didn't want to leave my little boy behind, crying because I loved him so much, crying because I was going to miss him, crying because he wasn't coming home after this, and crying because there was hope. Just crying. I felt cleansed and profoundly grateful for this experience.

I Feel...

Optimistic
Vulnerable
Empowered
Fragile
Yearning
Amused
Confident
Uneasy
Exhausted
Frustrated
Grateful
Sensitive
Hopeful

Family Visit Notes: The 4-Rs

TJ to Mom and Dad:

Regrets
- I regret losing my temper when I didn't feel heard in arguments.
- I regret lying to my parents about where I was and what I was doing.
- I regret not being a better role model for my sister.
- I regret continuing heavy use of weed even when I told my parents I'd stop.
- I regret not hearing my parents' side of things.
- I regret not spending more time with my parents.
- I regret not telling my dad I love him.
- I regret not opening up more to my parents.

Resentments
- I resent that my parents don't understand where my depression and anxiety come from.
- I resent my dad for working all the time, but I know it's for the best for our family.
- I resent my dad for losing his temper when I'd smoke weed at home.
- I resent my mom for not being able to get close to me because of my weed use.
- I resent my family for not sharing emotions with me.

Respects
- I respect my dad for having a strong will and never giving up.
- I respect my mom for trying to keep me healthy and happy.
- I respect my dad for working hard to provide for my family.
- I respect my mom for trying to keep everything in balance with my sister and me.
- I respect my dad for taking an interest in my life.

Requests
- I request that my dad and mom share their emotions rather than accuse me.
- I request that my dad and mom try to see my side as to why I used weed.

- I request that my parents continue to try to have family outings with me.
- I request that my parents continue to give love to me.

Mom to TJ:

Resentments

- I resent that you yelled profanities and called me terrible names.
- I resent how you said we "came down hard on you" and "didn't talk to you" when we had so many heart-to-heart talks with you.
- I resent that you said our relationship depends on my acceptance of you smoking dope.
- I resent that you wanted me to try drugs.
- I resent that you tried to make your little sister think that drugs were a positive thing and would tell her that while you were high.
- I resent that you downplayed your drug use.

Regrets

- I regret that I didn't send you to the wilderness sooner.
- I regret that you feel I didn't listen or talk to you enough.
- I regret that I was quick to lose my patience with you when you would lose your belongings.

Respects

- I respect the challenging work you are doing in the wilderness and how open you are to sharing your feelings.
- I respect your new verbal skills and your willingness to be open and honest.
- I respect how you apologized for your behavior.
- I respect your creativity and love of art and music.
- I respect that you're courteous and polite with adults.

Requests

- I request that you continue to keep the communication lines flowing.
- I request that you don't try to convince me that weed is the answer to your problems.
- I request that you keep your funny sense of humor.

- I request that you regulate your emotions without the use of substances when you come home.
- I request that you stay emotionally close to me.
- I request lots of hugs.
- I request that you continue to do the challenging work.

Dad to TJ:

Resentments
- I resent that you don't own your substance addiction and smoke weed rather than work on healthy coping strategies.
- I resent that you get dysregulated, and use swear words at us.
- I resent your inappropriate sharing of rap lyrics.
- I resent when you smoked weed around the house and how you exposed your sister to drug use.
- I resent your risky behavior.

Regrets
- I regret that my initial reaction was to toughen you up.
- I regret not handling specific situations in a mindful manner. (Bathroom incident on Labor Day)
- I regret making decisions/actions when I was angry.

Respects
- I respect your kindness.
- I respect your intelligence.
- I respect your creativity.
- I respect your personable traits.

Requests
- I request that you be understanding of our boundaries.
- I request that you work on being mindful.
- I request that you are truthful.

PHASE III: RETURN

Furthermore, we have not even to risk the adventure alone; for the heroes of all time have gone before us; the labyrinth is thoroughly known; we have only to follow the thread of the hero-path.

—Joseph Campbell, *The Hero with a Thousand Faces*

CHAPTER 10

SEIZING THE TREASURE

It is close to the end of a transformative journey. The hero has overcome trials in the woods and made incredible breakthroughs emotionally and physically.

Graduation

Mom's Narration:

Just when it seemed like our son was going to be in the woods forever, the time arrived for transition. We had known he would be in the mountains for at least ten to twelve weeks but did not receive a specific completion date until Badger thought he was ready. And when the exact day was finally revealed, *this mom was not ready!* I was finally getting comfortable with the whole situation and now felt unprepared to put my son back in the real world. The thought of him graduating made me both happy and sad. Still, the time to see my little boy face to face and hold him in my arms could not come soon enough. And then again, I was going to miss knowing he was in a place where he was fully supported and without access to substances. I was also going to miss refreshing my computer to find TJ's letters and being part of the support team of the program. And, we had less than two weeks to scramble for plane tickets.

Badger told us he would be out of town at the time of TJ's graduation, and I was disappointed at first. But he assured us that he had done what he was called for and was confident TJ was ready to fly on his own. There would be another primary therapist available to lead TJ through the transition.

TJ's Letter to His Grandparents:

Sunday, 4/22/18
Dear Nana and Saza,

I miss you so much. In the wilderness, it gets pretty hard because I think about home a lot. I've been putting in the hard work here. I moved to Air Phase, which means I am in the leadership direction. I'll get my own headlamp, I won't need to call out my name when taking a pee, and I have the job of checking my teammates' cups if they're dirty.

This week has been hard for me. I had to do a challenge to get to Air Phase, and I didn't know what was happening. A kid named G-dog came into my group from another team who was also due to move to Air, and the guides decided to challenge us by turning the two of us against each other by making us both Leaders of the Day. We each thought we were the only leaders. They gave G-dog and me a secret task and told us not to tell the team. At the end of the day, the guides told both of us to set up a ceremony to move the other person to Air. Both of us did it without question. We ended up completing the challenge and moved to Air Phase together. I'm happy to be getting closer to graduating from the program.

I am glad to hear everything is good at home.

I love you,
TJ

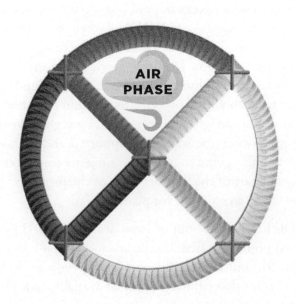

TJ's Letter of Accountability (LOA):

Sunday, 4/22/18
Dear Mom and Dad,

In this letter, my goal is to take full accountability for the ways I've hurt you in the past. I feel sad and disappointed I worried the family and hope that taking full responsibility for what I've done will be the first step to repairing our relationship. I also hope to help you understand why I made these choices by telling you what basic needs I was trying to meet by doing this and telling you how it affected me. My actions in the past have damaged my relationship with you, and the decisions I made did not align with my values or yours. One way I damaged our relationship is by lying to you that I was going to quit weed. During these times, I was trying to fulfill my need for freedom and fun, even though it led me to a loss of freedom. Though it was fun short term, it resulted in losing your trust in me, crossing my values of faith and trust.

Another way I damaged our relationship was aggressive communication with Mom and Beth. I was trying to have control over the situation by doing this, and I hurt you both. I'm working on getting better.

The last way I damaged our relationship was by sneaking out and lying about where I was. I was trying to satisfy my need for freedom by doing this, but in the end, I broke your trust, and it did not end up satisfying my needs.

My actions have also affected Nana and Saza. I broke their trust by taking their car out for a joy ride to try and satisfy my need for fun and excitement. I also smoked weed at their house and took beer from their fridge. I was trying to satisfy my need for freedom and escape, but I only compromised family trust and values.

Another person I hurt by my actions is my sister. I feel the most regret for what I did to her because I am her older brother and would like to be a good influence in her life. I am sorry that I would get high and talk to her about drugs. By doing this, I was trying to fulfill my need for belonging. I also let my friends hang around the house while they were high, and I wish I hadn't exposed her to that. When I destroyed my sister's playhouse with a hammer, I upset her. I now understand how the playhouse was still important to her because she and Dad built it together. I did this to get out my emotional pain. In reality, I scared her, broke connections with her, and made the whole family worry.

Thinking back on how I hurt you all is emotionally stressful because by doing these things, I was trying to satisfy my own selfish needs. In the future, I want to right these wrongs by sticking to the values I hold dear to me so I can show up consistently. I love and value you guys and hope you can forgive me for the actions I've done in the past so we can move on to the future and be a strong family.

Love,
TJ

Mom's Narration (LOA):

Tom and I were in shock and awe reading these words from TJ's Letter of Accountability (LOA). Did our son truly write this? It was hard to believe. But we knew TJ had come a long way. We hoped by him owning accountability for his actions, he would be released from shame and guilt.

When my mother and father read the LOA, it was the first time they learned that TJ drove their car without a license, smoked weed in their house, and took beer from their fridge. Not only did it take them by surprise that they had never noticed what went on in their home while he was there, but it also validated our decision to take him to wilderness instead of letting him move in with them. They had been reading TJ's letters each week, and it helped them understand his plight so they could offer him the kind of support he needed.

I read the letter aloud to TJ's sister, Beth. She listened quietly to her brother's words of remorse about his destruction of the playhouse and drug use around her. Although she nodded her head in acknowledgment, she was still not ready to forgive him. It was understandable that she needed more space.

Side Trip with the Sidelined Sister

We encouraged Beth, who was twelve years old at the time, to join us for the graduation trip. Hesitant to come with us because she was still trying to make sense of what had happened with her brother, she thankfully let us convince her. It was important to the whole family to be part of the process and for her to see what her brother had been up to all this time. There were amends to be made between the two of them, and we were hoping this would help them reconnect in some way.

TJ's behavior before wilderness, and the focus of our attention on him while he was away, profoundly affected Beth in multiple ways. It was hard for her to understand the difficult choices we had needed to make for her brother, and she harbored great resentment because of the attention required for his care. She felt as though her needs were overlooked because she was not a troublemaker. We had always tried to shield her from what was going on during the years prior, but nothing went over her head. Beth had been a silent and keen observer on the sidelines. It scared her when she noticed TJ was high. It upset her when she found his drug paraphernalia around the house. She was also still processing the fact that he took a hammer to her playhouse. TJ, in turn, had been resentful of the fact that his sister was often in the spotlight, such as taking on big roles as a musical theater performer.

We enticed Beth with a fun side trip to scenic towns in Colorado and Utah before TJ's graduation. I labeled it as a necessary and educational homeschool "field trip." Tom and I wanted to put the focus solely on her beforehand, so she would feel special and supported. The three of us spent time exploring quaint and rustic mountain towns, took a train tour to the historic town of Silverton, and visited the Ancestral Puebloan cave dwellings of Mesa Verde National Park. It was a great adventure before the reunion.

TJ's Field Journal:
Thursday, 4/26/18

Today I got mail from my family, which was super heartwarming. I got a pocket frisbee, disposable cameras, pictures of my family, and letters. This was the first time in a long time I felt that everyone in my family was ready to support and love me. In feeling this, the emotions I experienced were happiness, love, gratitude, and peace, but I also felt regret. I felt happy because I got the physical things, which are awesome. Grateful because I appreciate the thought that was put into this gift. Loved because I got to see pictures of my family and letters. Regretful that I broke my family's trust. Lastly, at peace, because I realized I'm going to spend time with my family again soon.

I found out I'm going to a nonrestrictive aftercare in Utah. I'm grateful my parents put consideration into my future because I see the future being bright.

Letter to TJ from Mom:

Saturday, 4/28/18
Dear TJ,

I feel excited, optimistic, and joyful when I think about your upcoming graduation from wilderness. I feel this way because I know you have worked so hard and deserve to celebrate the incredible things you have accomplished. I also feel this way because I will be hugging you again soon. At this moment, I am going to take a deep breath and think about the days to come until I see you.

After sharing this I-feel, I will organize a suitcase of your belongings [for you] to take on your next step to aftercare so you will have clean clothes to wear. I imagine you'll be happy to wear your favorite t-shirt and a pair of jeans while we take a road trip through Utah. We can stop along the way to eat in restaurants and see the sites. I'm looking forward to spending time with you, listening to music, and hearing all the stories you must share with us.

I love you so much and will see you soon!

Love,
Mom

Letter to TJ from Dad:

Saturday, 4/28/18
Dear TJ,

By the time you read this, I am sure you will be on cloud nine and counting the days until graduation. We are all looking forward to seeing you next week and being part of your big day!

I want to share that I am proud of you and all the great work you have done. I now know that it was incredibly challenging physically but particularly emotionally and mentally. When we made the decision on wilderness, we were confident that this would be a broad experience. I am sure the first couple of weeks were rough for you, and more than once, I worried about our decision. Hearing that you had to make your own spoon, or you had to use your fingers to eat, was an eye-opener! I am sure there is pride in all your hard skill accomplishments—what a confidence builder! More importantly, Wilderness Therapy turned out to be much deeper on the introspective/emotional work than I had imagined. I did not understand what a large part of the experience that work would be, and now I am incredibly grateful for that. And I am particularly amazed and humbled by the amount of effort you invested. It is truly awesome.

I am excited about the next step, moving to aftercare. Of course, we miss you so much and we wish the next step were home, but we understand that the therapeutic boarding school is critical to long-term success. Moving from wilderness will be a tremendous change, so my request to you is that you ease into it and remember all the challenging work you have put into this journey. You and Mom will get to have some quality time together on the way to aftercare. Soon I will come for a weekend of one-on-one time, which I'm looking forward to!

I love you, and I am so proud of the positive energy and attitude you have put into your work.

Love,
Dad

Final Wilderness Letter from TJ to Parents:

Monday, 4/30/18
Dear Mom and Dad,

This week has been heartwarming and eye-opening for me. I got to see the new kids go through what I went through at the beginning of my stay. It's sad and curious to see what that looks like coming from the other side of it. I got to give the boys some insight into what it is like when you have been here as long as I have. It feels good when you're the one reassuring everyone instead of people convincing you it's gonna be okay.

Being a leader for the team is an awesome feeling but also kind of nerve-racking due to freshies looking to me to see how things work. I feel passionate about making this culture awesome before I leave, so I try to put in as much work as possible. It's cool that I've got all the hard skills down. The new guides are even taking tips from me on stuff like bow drilling. Senior guides have become like buddies to me. One of the guides, Chris, who lives around here, is one of my favorites. He recently killed two sheep and fed sixty people with them. After I'm done with residential treatment, I hope to see him again and maybe do a backpacking trip with him.

I'm anxious for the next steps after wilderness. Though everything right now is exciting, I find it hard to think that in a matter of a week or two, I'll be back in society. It feels like I've been here all my life but at the same time seems like a short time.

I think I'm having a phone call with the aftercare today so I can learn more about it. Also, they are going to let me have a call with my friend Jimmy. I'm nervous about it. I don't know what to say to him, and at the same time, there's so much to talk about.

This week I'm trying to move to Fire Phase. It would be an honor to get to that position. I'm excited to see you again. I love you and miss you so much.*

Love,
TJ

*The Fire Phase was not a requirement to graduate the program, and only select students achieve this level. TJ graduated in The Air Phase.

TJ's Field Journal—Grad Prep Notes:

I-feel Statements for My Parents:

For Dad:

Positive: I feel happy, hopeful, grateful because I get to see you soon and talk about what's happening at home.

Belief: I value family, and I want to learn what has happened in your life and get closer to you.

Intention: Finish off the week strong and try my best at graduation.

Request: Be open and transparent with me.

Hard: I feel sad, regretful, and hopeful when I think back on our relationship in the past and see that we were so distant. My belief is that I value family, and I regret not trying to be closer to you. I also value love, and what I had been doing did not support a loving relationship. My intention for myself is to be open and honest, so we can have a better relationship. My request for you is to do the same.

For Mom:

Positive: I feel happy, grateful, and excited. I feel this way when I think about the road trip we are about to take together. My belief as to why I feel this way is because I love you, and I'm grateful I get to spend time with you after being away from you for so long. My intention for myself is to do my best to explain what my time here was like. My request for you is to arrange more time for us to be together.

Hard: I feel sad, resentful, and nostalgic. I feel this way when I think back on the times when we said things that hurt each other, and I'm sad we had to do that. My belief as to why I feel this way is because I value peace, love, and family, and during those times, it wasn't peaceful or loving. My intention for myself is to apologize and let you know I love and appreciate you. My request for you is to do the same.

Mom's Narration:

Reuniting
Tuesday, 5/8/18

After our vacation with Beth touring the Four Corners region, we were ready to begin the quest of transitioning TJ from the woods to the real world. We met with the field staff below the base camp and were warmly greeted by a group of families whose children were also graduating. So much excitement was buzzing in the air among the families, knowing we were all about to see our kids soon. We proceeded to follow the guides behind a caravan of cars toward camp, driving alongside everlasting stretches of horse and cattle ranches. Eventually, there was a sharp turn before the entrance to a private drive off of the main road. It morphed into an unpaved twisting path which cut through grassy meadows. The sun was shining, and the mood inside our car was upbeat. Beth was picking out tunes from her music playlist as the car bounced along, blowing clouds of dust behind us. Eventually, the beaten path started to incline toward tall and shady pine trees.

Once we arrived at the camp, we unloaded our overnight bags and reassembled with the other families under an umbrella of evergreens. The staff reminded us to lock away our cell phones, watches, and jewelry. For the next two days, we were going to experience what it was like to live like our children had for the past three months. (TJ humbled us later by pointing out that our version of outdoor therapy was more like the Ritz-Carlton, compared to his.)

The staff had us gather around in a circle and led us through deep-breathing exercises and a feelings check-in. Mine sounded something like this:

My body is tired, I picture my son smiling, my heart is light, I feel connected.

It was a much-needed pause. I felt eager and giddy, knowing we were close to TJ. The guides went ahead to escort our group up a trail and along a wooded path. It was quiet and tranquil, except for the wind blowing through the trees and the crunching sound from our feet on the dusty trail.

As we continued our short hike, we eventually turned a corner and reached an embankment. I raised my head and noticed silhouettes of grungy-looking young kids scattered about in the distance. They were unmoving and silently waiting there for us. I knew TJ was among them, but I could not make out which one he was at first because the sun was shining in our direction, and their backs were facing us. The sight was luminous. When these heroes of the wilderness sensed us behind them and heard our footsteps, one by one they started gradually turning around to search for their loved ones.

Tom and I sped up our pace. I squinted to zero in on the scene, scanning the area for my son. Then, without a doubt, I detected his long and lanky stature. On his head was that same semi-crooked tan bucket hat with a chin strap draping haphazardly. His smile stretched from ear to ear. We approached him with our arms wide open. I hugged him so hard. I did not ever want to let go. All the worries that had been haunting me for the last several years seemed to melt away. It was an emotional moment. There was so much love and so much hope. Our whole family stayed there, reunited, in each other's arms. We lost track of time, along with the realization of where we were and why we were there.

Bitters and Sweets

The spring air was fresh, and the smell of the pine trees intoxicating. TJ, Tom, Beth, and I settled into a campsite with a tarp shelter set up especially for us. It was isolated from the rest of the base. The feeling was peaceful. We were given some alone time as a family to reconnect without staff or other students around.

Under the shelter, the four of us stretched out on sleeping mats, reclining against our duffel bags. We basked in the pine-scented air, inhaling the woods, and snacked on food similar to the weekly personal rations TJ had been given each week: pears, dry oats, and a large block of dense white cheese. As we restored ourselves, Beth took out her sketchbook to draw some of the sights around us, and I recorded some notes in my journal. TJ told us about how he and another senior student were asked to become the mentors of a team of boys who recently arrived at camp. He loved being in the position of showing new students the ropes.

Before the pre-graduation dinner, TJ wanted to teach Beth how to bust a coal using the "tandem method." She was intrigued. A little ways away from the shelter, TJ instructed Beth on how to prepare the bow drill set on the forest floor. Tom and I watched the two of them work out who would hold the bow and who would hold the spindle. Once they set it up properly, we could hear the rattling sound of sticks rubbing together between the cord as TJ held the spindle steady with the rock socket. It looked cumbersome, and it took them several tries, but their collaboration eventually produced a glowing coal. We cheered their success! They brought the fireboard to proudly show us black smoldering powder, and we could smell the burning wood.

Later that evening, we all walked along a pathway through the woods that led us to TJ's team campsite. The boys and field guides were expecting us. They seemed happy to see fresh faces and welcomed us around the glowing fire. TJ told us that the students liked it when members of the group graduate, because the food was prepared extra special. I enjoyed observing how he interacted with his tribe. They seemed to be in sync with laughing and joking around. You would never guess these boys were suffering with complex issues, or why they had landed in Wilderness Therapy in the first place.

Besides the ceremonies and rituals led by the team during the dinner, what I remembered most were what they called *Bitters and Sweets*. Everyone took turns voicing sentiments about the graduates as the fire twisted and crackled, making the evening seem magical. The *Sweets* were sentimental or funny stories from the field, and the *Bitters* were honest concerns. Each parent and student voiced real, raw, honest words. Then the teammates gave parting dialogue, expressed with such maturity and feeling I was moved beyond belief. It was obvious their shared experiences and personal battles had resulted in a deep connection. If only I had a recording of their heartfelt sentiments. It was an unforgettable experience.

At bedtime, our family snuggled up under the shelter together, nestled in thick sleeping bags under the stars. It was an exhausting day, but we were not ready to sleep. Beth pulled out her *Diary of a Wimpy Kid* book. It was one of TJ's favorites. The two of them read it together using the light from their headlamps, laughing with each other. TJ was thrilled to read something other than therapy assignments on his last night. It was refreshing seeing the two of them interact in the simplest way. Things were not perfectly resolved between them because of this trip, but it was good enough for the moment. Time would likely heal their differences.

I remained sleepless that night, replaying events that had transpired in the last few days, last few months, and last few years. Despite the difficulties we faced, my heart filled with gratitude for what we had accomplished.

Graduation Day
Wednesday, 5/9/18

Throughout the Wilderness Therapy journey, I had been capturing my thoughts and observations in my leather-bound diary. I found journaling to be an important healing tool during this process. Nevertheless, for these final days at camp the journal stayed tucked away in my duffel bag so I could focus on being in the moment. The details of the graduation ceremony are hazy, but I do remember feeling an exuberant buzz of positive spirits as I sat next to TJ in a circle under an open tent with the other graduates and their families. I took in the beauty of our surroundings and inhaled fresh smells of the woods around us. There was a cleansing sage smudging, a string of colorful flags flapping in the blue sky above us, and the sounds of a metal gong vibrating through the air. In that moment, a jumble of feelings stirred inside of me. I took hold of both TJ and Beth's hands and squeezed them. Any resentment and fear I had held inside disappeared along with the sage smoke swirling up into the atmosphere. It was replaced by great hope and anticipation for the future. My heart only held room for gratitude, love, and respect for our son, who had completed a life-altering journey.

TJ's Reflection on the Wilderness Therapy Graduation:

Saturday, 4/17/2021

Graduation was an amazing experience. Good food, seeing my family again and celebrating with my team, whom I considered my brothers. What more can you ask for after spending three months in the middle of nowhere?

Before my graduation, the program was making a move to a cooler location for the summer. On the van ride to the new campsite, the guides brought along a speaker and let us play whatever songs we liked. I had not heard recorded music or rode in a car since the day I arrived in the woods. Never had I been so glad to be jamming out.

During the grad ceremony, I was pinching myself to make sure I wasn't dreaming. The near three months I spent in the desert were pivotal moments in my life. I cannot imagine where I would have been without going through that experience. There were many moments that sucked to the fullest. But there was a certain point, once I learned to accept the situation and look all around me at what was once a barren wasteland and think, "Man, this place is beautiful." There were many difficult moments. Trials to test my psyche and perceived or profoundly serious hardships in the wilderness. But mentality was everything. The Navy Seals have the best phrase for this: "Embrace the suck."

Wilderness was just the first step in changing the risky behaviors I struggled with, which were depression, anxiety, and cannabis abuse, to cope with the two. After the graduation ceremony I said final goodbyes to my teammates and guides. Badger could not be there, but I am so grateful to him. He helped me make important breakthroughs and taught me how to see things within myself like no other therapist could do.

My mother and I hit the road on the way to the aftercare program. The reality of the situation hit me harder than when I got to the wilderness. I was tired of feeling stuck in programs, sad I couldn't see my family, afraid and uncertain of what was to come at the aftercare program. I broke down in the bathroom on the way there, feeling overwhelmed with the whole thing.

ROAD TO AFTERCARE

The wilderness setting evolves into an ordinary world *for the hero as he becomes accustomed to a lifestyle without electricity and running water. It is time to launch into a new and different* special world *so he can continue his path toward lasting wellness. He crosses the threshold to aftercare, where he finds himself a new set of mentors and road bumps to navigate. This time it is different because he starts his new journey on top of a mountain. Fortunately, he can see clearly and is better equipped to handle the emotional ups and downs ahead.*

Goodbye to Woods

Mom's Narration:

With hearts full of gratitude, we said our farewells to the staff and to the families we had met at the graduation. TJ organized his belongings and rolled them up in a tarp to take with him. The bow drill set he handled with extreme care. He donated his backpack for use by the next wilderness hero, who would earn the privilege of carrying it.

I knew we would be traveling in close quarters with a strong-smelling wilder-child. And boy, did he smell! It was a good thing I made sure to bring a deodorant stick and a clean set of clothes to change into. He was thrilled to swap the worn-out blue T-shirt and cargo pants uniform issued by the program for a fresh shirt and pair of shorts from home. A shower, shave, and haircut were also much needed, but that would have to wait. We promised to grant him his wish of a family meal in a restaurant as soon as we left camp. He had been craving cheeseburgers and fries since he was called to adventure.

A staff member approached TJ and gave him a box filled with his belongings, which had been stored in a warehouse since the first day he arrived. They were forgotten items from the *ordinary world*. He chose not to open the box from his past for the time being; instead, he placed it in the trunk of the rental car next to his rolled-up tarp. It was time for TJ to begin his new journey.

Although the family was on this wilderness high from the past few days, reality set in that we couldn't take TJ home with us. We understood that enrolling him in therapeutic boarding school was important to securing long-term recovery. I will never forget an analogy shared with us at the aftercare parent weekend seminar, led by the family services coordinator.

When students graduate from outdoor therapy, they resemble tiny sprouts, tender and susceptible to the elements. Aftercare works as a greenhouse, giving the sprouts more time to grow and strengthen before they are put out into the garden.

On the Road Again

As we pulled away from the woods to descend toward the real world with TJ in the back seat, I was reminded of the day we brought him home from the hospital seventeen years ago when he was a tender newborn, wrapped in a blanket like a burrito in his infant carrier. My thoughts and feelings were like the thoughts and feelings I had on that eventful day. I wanted to shield him from the big bad world outside. Tom and I were given a heads up by Badger and our educational consultant that TJ would experience somewhat of a culture shock re-entering society; they recommended that we keep the itinerary simple.

Once in the town below, we came upon a small roadhouse pub in the southwestern town of Cortez. It was one of a few restaurants in the area that claimed to have the best burgers in the Four Corners. It had Harley-Davidsons parked out front, and as we walked in, I saw a saloon-like bar in the back with locals perched on the stools. What a contrast it was for TJ to enter a place with music playing, restaurant chatter, and the smell of greasy cooking, after three months of living in such an incredibly arcadian wilderness.

TJ told us the sounds overwhelmed him and made him light-headed. I wondered whether we should go someplace else, but when I suggested finding a quieter place, he said he wanted to stay because he was too hungry to wait any longer. Plus, there was a jukebox that further lured him inside.

We took our seats in a booth and studied the menus. I warned TJ about his eyes being bigger than his stomach and to be careful not to eat too much, too fast. He was used to eating only clean and simple meals. I felt like a new mother feeding her baby solid food for the first time.

Our server arrived at the table, and TJ's face lit up as he gave her his order. "I'll have BBQ wings, a double cheeseburger, a basket of fries, and a Sprite, please. And by the way, I just got back from a three-month expedition in the wilderness." He beamed with pride. She raised her eyebrows in amusement and seemed impressed.

Taking one glance at him, it was believable. He looked like Shaggy from *Scooby-Doo* with his thin goatee and dirty hair covering his ears. "The wilder look," he called it. He was enjoying this new status as a rugged explorer.

As we waited for our food to arrive, TJ and his sister put money in the jukebox and played a game of pool. It was sweet watching them having fun together.

The hamburgers and wings did not disappoint. They were fat and juicy, with a side of thickly sliced pickles and homemade potato chips. TJ could not decide what to stuff in his mouth first. He went back and forth, taking bites of the wings in one hand and the burger in the other. His eyes closed with pleasure as he took in the flavors. He said he thought it was the best food he had ever tasted. During the meal, we did not talk about aftercare or his future. We were just an ordinary family enjoying each other's company around a table as so many normal families do.

After our dinner, we left the restaurant to drop TJ's dad and sister off at their car rental so we could go our separate ways. The two of them needed to venture back home, while TJ and I had a long drive to our first overnight stop on the way to his aftercare.

Moab

We took the road north toward Moab on a desolate two-lane high-way, leaving the woods behind us. I felt so connected to TJ after the graduation and was looking forward to having him all to myself on this two-day trip. I intended for our time together to be light and fun after months of intensive therapeutic work.

The first order of business for TJ was to select an iTunes playlist from my phone. He was champing at the bit to hear what new songs had been released while he was off-grid. Tom and I had laid out firm ground-work for TJ around electronics before he left the mountains. Badger had helped TJ process the fact that he would not get his phone back until he earned it, much later, in his aftercare program. He grudgingly accepted using my device, and only for listening to music and calling family members.

We had a pleasant drive through the southwestern farmlands, dotted with horses and bison roaming the fields. It was not so pleasant for me having to hear rap music blasting with the windows rolled down. I admit to enjoying watching TJ's excitement over his temporary freedom, so I put up with his music choices through gritted teeth. My only condition was the lyrics needed to be non-explicit, which meant skipping to the next song more than once. TJ would always ask me if I liked this song or that song, and I was glad he at least cared about my opinion. Par-ticipating in conversations about his favorite rappers was another way for me to connect with him. He analyzed everything about the music, from the beats to the facts about each music artist. On the plus side, I found it to be a good distraction from thinking about dropping him off at aftercare.

Cutting through the desert canyons toward Moab, I focused on the stunning scenery. The display of dramatic red rock formations was rem-iniscent of *Roadrunner* cartoons. TJ expressed wanting to stop and set up camp for the night. I thought he was kidding at first and went along by saying, "Okay, sure, let's do it!" But he took me seriously. When I mentioned that we did not have sleeping bags or food, he said we had everything we needed in the trunk of the car ... a bow drill, a tarp, and the skills he had to live off the land. I could not believe I was hearing these words coming from my son, who had never liked going camping.

The idea of veering off the road to sleep under the stars lasted for only a hot minute because TJ began feeling indigestion from his burger and hot wings. He turned off the music and reclined his seat. We quietly watched the sky change to bright orange and fuchsia, reflecting a pleasant glow on the steep cliffs. His "wilderness high" started fading as fast as the sun was setting on the horizon, and from there emerged an overwhelming surge of emotions.

He talked about wanting to go home and how he was feeling sad, lost, confused, anxious, stressed, and exhausted. I wanted to fix it but didn't know what to do except validate his feelings. No matter how prepared I was for him to mentally take this dive, my stomach tightened and my knuckles turned white against the steering wheel. Fear set in, and I worried that the magnificent work he had done was all going to be lost.

I suggested that he call the program exit support team who were available to him, but he didn't want to. Instead, he took a deep breath and announced, "I'm going to bust an *I-feel.*" I don't recall exactly what he said, but I remember it being intentional and thoughtful. He took the initiative to express his emotions, and I was honored to listen. I reflected his long-winded *I-feel* back to him by trying to repeat the essence of it. Then I asked him if he felt heard. He filled in a few missing pieces and made sure I didn't forget anything. When we were done, he said he felt heard. It was like a balloon had popped, and we both felt a little better.

We arrived in Moab by nightfall, and TJ went straight to the hotel bathroom to fill the bathtub with hot water. I gave him a package of bubble bath, purchased ahead of time, and left him to soak with his music for the next hour. When he was done, we both laughed at the brown ring left around the tub as the swampy water drained. I noticed he didn't shave his mustache and chin whiskers. He told me he wanted to indefinitely preserve his "wilder-look."

Emerging from the bathroom looking refreshed with clean hair and clipped fingernails, TJ jumped onto the bed and lay back on the pillows with his hands folded behind his head. He marveled at how comfortable it felt. Then he turned on the TV and flipped through the channels but quickly turned it off because it was too stimulating. I let him use my phone to make phone calls to family members. When he was ready to call it a night, he made his bed on the floor using the comforter. The mattress was too soft for him.

Aftercare Arrival
Thursday, 5/10/18

We ate a hearty breakfast the next day at the hotel buffet on the outdoor patio. It had an incredible view of rocky red cliffs in the distance. TJ filled his plate high with stacks of pancakes, eggs, and bacon. It was more than his stomach could handle, but he relished every bite.

I found a place in town for TJ to get a haircut. While he was draped in a smock with his freshly cut locks tumbling to the ground, he proudly told the barber about how he survived a three-month expedition in the Utah mountains. I was entertained as I listened to him tell stories of his adventures to a total stranger.

The next leg of our journey was about a five-hour drive toward a suburb of Salt Lake City. This gave us plenty of time for more rap music and other bonding opportunities. It also provided time for our conversation to become progressively rockier. TJ started stressing out about going to aftercare and argued his case for going home by pointing out a luxury sports car passing us on the road. He thought we were wasting our money and should purchase one of *those* instead. But then he told me a hair-raising story which did not help his case for going home.

The incident he described had happened before he went to woods, when he stood on the roof of a high-rise building in downtown LA and contemplated jumping. Fortunately, a security guard found him leaning over the edge and tackled him to the ground, preventing the unthinkable. Hearing TJ tell me this story had me shuddering and feeling numb. I expressed to him that I would forgo a luxury car any day to keep him safe. Even more so, I made it clear that his dad and I would spend our every dime in doing so.

Once TJ and I made it to the suburban town where the program was located, we stopped for a last meal together in a local restaurant. As we ate, the mood was somewhat somber, but we tried to joke around, to distract each other from what was to come. When he started telling me how nervous he felt, I listened and calmly said, "I hear you are nervous and know it will be hard. Remember how much your dad and I love you." During most of the meal, I held up strongly. But then the tide turned, and I broke into tears. We took some deep breaths together, and then TJ put his arm around me.

When we arrived at the therapeutic boarding school, the director of the program was in the front yard waiting to greet us. The home was a white-painted, wood-clad traditional dwelling nestled in a quiet suburban neighborhood at the foot of the Wasatch Mountain Range. I had already been there on a tour a few weeks before, so I knew what to expect.

I would describe the campus as a sober fraternity house. It had skateboarding ramps outside, snowboarding equipment hanging on hooks in the entry, a ping-pong table in the family room, a pet bearded dragon, and a separate schoolroom in the back. There were two therapists in the house assigned to about fourteen boys. TJ's therapist had an office inside the home. However, most of the therapy happened during the daily activities and out-of-town trips.

During my tour, the director introduced me to some of the current students who happened to be hanging around the house that day. This gave me an understanding of the boys who would be living with TJ. I sat in a room with them and had an honest conversation about their experiences at the home without any staff around. All had come directly from different outdoor therapy programs. Although none would have chosen to be there, they seemed happy enough.

The kids told me about how they kept busy with trips and outdoor sports. Every Friday night, they were rewarded with going to dinner and a movie if in good standing. They shared with me how the level system worked. If rules were broken or if they relapsed, privileges would be lost, and they would be bumped down to what was called the "poser" level. The students worked hard to level up and gain more independence. Some eventually went out and applied for jobs in town. The ultimate freedom was to earn their cell phones back.

Since the therapeutic boarding school wasn't a lock-down type of facility, TJ had the ability not only to thrive but also to backtrack. Backtracking is considered a growing opportunity. Although the boys were supervised around the clock by rotating shifts of daytime and nighttime staff, the program was considered to be a "loose container." Because of this, the facility did not accept anyone who had a history of running away.

TJ and I exited the car and walked up the driveway. There were several rowdy-looking teenagers riding around on skateboards and playing basketball. TJ seemed shell-shocked from the burst of activity going on around him and didn't say much. One of the boys broke away from the group and introduced himself as Nate. He was going to be TJ's roommate and mentor. With a friendly demeanor, Nate helped TJ with his belongings and showed him to his room.

I didn't stay long, as it was exceedingly difficult for both of us to say goodbye. Before I left, I put framed photos of our family and one of Tango next to his bed. TJ was withdrawn and fighting back tears. It was one of the hardest days of my life, leaving him there.

Ninety Days of Darkness

Transitioning from Wilderness Therapy, where your child goes from zero to hero in a matter of three months, is a powerful, mountaintop experience. However, going back to the *ordinary world* and entering the next phase of an aftercare program was a big letdown—for both TJ and for us as parents.

I would compare Wilderness Therapy to riding the Goliath rollercoaster at Six Flags Magic Mountain for the first time. The buildup of anticipation is overwhelming. Feelings of terror as we gradually clickity-clack up the steep incline, wishing all the way that we could abort the mission. At the summit, we realize there is no going back. Then a brief pause. Palms sweating. Feet dangling. The next thing we know, we are flying downhill, going upside down and around the loop-de-loops with our hearts pounding. It's wild, scary, and fast. Then the ride comes to a screeching halt. We are all completely exhausted from the adrenaline rush but glad for it.

Aftercare was more like riding Pinocchio's Daring Journey at Disneyland ten times in a row. It's dark inside, slower, and much less intense. It goes in circles, takes some turns, dips, and bumps. Forward and backward. Backward and forward. It's anticlimactic and seems never-ending.

There is this darkness phase after riding the Goliath known as the *Ninety Days of Darkness*. It's about a three-month period of time when students are down in the dumps after their transition from wilderness and are most vulnerable to relapse. Being aware of this phase helped TJ's dad and me remain resolute and calm instead of reacting in fear that TJ would revert to his old coping habits. It also confirmed our decision to enroll TJ in aftercare because he would be in a continued therapeutic environment during such a sensitive and critical time.

For the first few months at aftercare, TJ begged to come home or even go back to the wilderness instead of being at the boarding school for the rest of the school year. But after we had invested so much time, money, emotion, and—most of all—energy into TJ's recovery, we could not take the chance of him coming home and going back to his old coping tactics. He needed to give his brain a chance to grow and mature, free from the damaging substances that created this whole incredible chapter in our lives. We had to be patient and stick to our guns when he resisted.

The part about aftercare Tom and I found most difficult was that TJ had the opportunity to complain about his problems in the moment, via phone calls and visits, without first taking time to work through them. When he was in wilderness, he had a chance to process how he was feeling while on long hikes and would only write about what he was still hanging onto in his weekly letters.

Prior to the family therapy and social calls at the TBS, we excitedly anticipated hearing TJ's voice. Often, though, the calls left us with hearts sinking from listening to his protests. It was excruciating not to be able to fix his problems. Tom and I relied on our new communication skills we acquired at the wilderness program. For example, TJ would say he was frustrated at living in a house full of boys. We took notice, validated, reflected, and validated some more. He missed home and complained about the rules of the aftercare house. We listened, validated, reflected, and validated some more ...

Light at the End of the Tunnel

About three months into aftercare, TJ made it past the darkness phase, and the gray clouds lifted. He gained motivation to do the work and find enjoyment in the activities the program had to offer. He was kept busy with mountain biking, wakeboarding, climbing, and other outdoor sports. He also had the chance to earn some money doing odd jobs for the program.

As a result of missing the entire second semester of his junior year while he was at wilderness, TJ needed to get back on track with his school credits. The therapeutic boarding school played an especially significant role by providing much-needed academic support, while having access to therapy built in. He was even able to take SAT prep courses and, to my surprise, looked forward to them. This was because he enjoyed time away from the house while he was driven an hour to Salt Lake City by the program staff—who he liked spending time with—to attend the classes. Not only did TJ catch up, but he applied himself and finished his last year of high school a semester early.

I missed connecting with TJ through his letters. He was always so good at expressing himself and his feelings in writing. But while at aftercare, we were able to speak to him on the phone for weekly family therapy sessions and social calls. He eventually earned the use of his cell phone and could talk to us anytime he wanted.

At the beginning of TJ's time at the boarding school, his dad and I made trips out to visit. We tried to make our time together light and fun by exploring the town, eating out, golfing, or renting ATVs. As TJ worked his way through the levels of the program, he gained the opportunity for a home visit, where he would leave the structured environment of aftercare to practice his new skills. It was a milestone to be dropped off at the airport by the program staff and make the journey unaccompanied. These homestays gave him a chance to practice putting his toes in the water and testing his boundaries with us. Tom and I worked on holding those boundaries by applying our new parenting and communication skills. Whenever it was time for TJ to go back to the TBS, I would stay strong while dropping him off at the airport and then cry in the car all the way home.

Leading up to these visits, during family therapy calls we would discuss which friends were okay for TJ to spend time with. The ones who we knew would not be supportive of his recovery were called "red friends." His crew of friends was primarily yellow and red, so naturally, we allowed him to see only "green" friends. TJ was happy to see his buddies again but found that it was hard to relate to them after the journey he had been on. He said it was like viewing them through "different goggles." We were also relieved that TJ had matured and had little interest in reconnecting with the red friends, sparing us from the nerve-wracking experience many families have when their child first returns home from aftercare.

After a year of wilderness and aftercare, TJ made his hero's return home, just in time to celebrate the holidays and his graduation from high school with our family. Even though the residential program was anticlimactic after the powerful life-changing experiences in wilderness, it allowed TJ to mature and finish his senior year safe and substance-free.

TJ's Narration:

Friday, 7/23/21
Although I do not look back on aftercare very fondly—don't get me wrong, there were fun things we did, awesome people I met, etc.—it did allow me time away from home so I could avoid immediate temptation. During wilderness, you go through sort of a death, then you are reborn into this new person ... but you're still the same person.

Once you make it through the wilderness, you have this sense of bliss and knowledge of yourself, and you feel like you've accomplished this massive thing. And then you get plopped back into this "regular-ish" life, and you don't know what you're supposed to do because you have all these things you've overcome. It makes it especially hard if you don't have aftercare to keep you from messing up. But yeah, it takes a long time to see the true benefits of the wilderness. You yourself are changing incrementally and you don't see the change until you've been out of it for a long time. I think of how I was back then, then think, *look at where I am now*. It's the same thing with any journey because you are learning, and you are going through these steps, and don't see until you're there. Wilderness Therapy is a mind-manifesting experience.

CHAPTER 12

THE HERO'S RETURN

A triumphant return home is the last step in the hero's transformative journey. He brings with him an elixir of enlightenment and hope for the future. The journey not only changes him, but he becomes Master of Two Worlds.

Homecoming

Mom's Narration:

Saturday, 12/22/18

Tango, our much-loved family dog, sat with me on the front porch steps, prepared to jump all over his favorite person the moment TJ arrived home from the airport with his dad. We were all excitedly anticipating his homecoming after Wilderness Therapy and therapeutic boarding school. Once they pulled into the driveway and the car door opened, Tango dashed from the porch and into TJ's open arms, his tail and entire body wiggling. As Dorothy from *The Wizard of Oz* once put it after clicking her sparkly red shoes, "There's no place like home."

The house was decked out with black and gold graduation swag to celebrate TJ's earning his high school diploma while at TBS. A few of his friends from his *ordinary world* joined our family for a small celebration dinner. TJ tried his best to integrate his new wisdom by describing to his friends what the *special world* was all about, but of course, they did not have the context to understand. It was still a mystery to them how he had disappeared and come back as this mythical creature who could make fire with sticks.

This was not the way we had imagined our son finishing high school, but we were thankful for the way it turned out. TJ learned more important lessons from his wilderness and aftercare experiences than he ever could have if he'd remained inside a classroom, attended a prom or Grad Night, and continued the unhealthy path he had been on. Instead, he earned an emotional education degree. The program changed him in the most profound ways, forming an impression that will stay with him throughout his life. The essential life skills he learned were also tools he needed to regulate himself without self-medicating or self-harming.

Wilderness Therapy gave this hero the power of resilience.

Step Down Program

Although it may sound like TJ's story neatly ended with his home-coming, he had a whole new journey to take, along with another set of trials and tribulations. The next stage began with his emergence into adulthood. TJ wanted to exercise the right to make his own decisions, but we knew he was not yet ready to commit to sobriety long-term. Quitting weed and other substances was not something he had initiated in the first place. After investing so much time, energy, and our personal finances, Tom and I couldn't afford to take any chances. We played the cards we had left to keep our son's developing brain sober while he was still under our wing; the only control we had was a grip on the purse strings and a firm set of boundaries.

With deep breaths and our hearts full of hope, we offered TJ our financial support if he agreed to continue his treatment by moving into a step down program that incorporated the twelve steps of AA. We figured he was not going to be thrilled about this, and our assumption was right. He was angry and balked at the idea of going to another "program." We made sure he understood that no matter what decision he made, we would always support him with our unconditional love.

After mulling things over for a few days and realizing the other options were to couch-surf or check into a homeless shelter, he decided to make the move into a young adult sober living house near his community college.

To this day, Tom and I are extremely grateful TJ accepted our terms of parental support, albeit reluctantly. We understand many young adults take the other direction when there's a fork in the road and experience more rock bottoms before there's a desire to make internal shifts.

The Transtheoretical Model

Whenever Tom and I felt anxious about our son taking steps backward while he was at the therapeutic boarding school or the step down program, we reminded ourselves that regression is a normal and expected part of the process. There is a behavioral model conceptualized by psychologists James O. Prochaska and Carlo Di Clemente named the Transtheoretical Model, or Stages of Change. It is a framework to describe six identifiable stages that individuals go through while trying to change a behavior. The idea was originally intended for smoking cessation patients but can translate to any type of negative habit.

While attempting to make a change, when relapse occurs, one can still jump back into any stage at any time (abandoning the change). The cycle will go on and on until the change eventually happens. Failure or regression is normal and allows opportunity for growth and learning. Below are the steps we were made aware of:

Stages of Change

- Precontemplation: Not yet acknowledging there is problem behavior that needs to be changed

- Contemplation: Acknowledging problem behavior but not committed to making a change

- Preparation: Getting ready to change

- Action Phase: Changing behavior

- Maintenance: Maintaining the behavior change

- Relapse: Returning to older behaviors and abandoning the new change

THE STAGES OF CHANGE CYCLE

PRECONTEMPLATION
NO INTENTION OF
CHANGING BEHAVIOR.

CONTEMPLATION
AWARE A PROBLEM
EXISTS.
NO COMMITMENT TO
ACTION.

PREPARATION
INTENT UPON
TAKING ACTION.

ACTION
ACTIVE MODIFICATION
OF BEHAVIOR.

MAINTENANCE
SUSTAINED CHANGE-
NEW BEHAVIOR
REPLACES OLD.

RELAPSE
FALL BACK INTO OLD
PATTERNS OF
BEHAVIOR.

When relapse occurs, one can still jump back into any stage at any time.

This Stages of Change Model diagram is adapted from the Stages of Change Model (also called the Transtheoretical Model) by Prochaska and Di Clemente (1983).

Summary of the Hero's Next Journey

Upon seizing the treasure in the wilderness and then at after-care, TJ is called to his next adventure, on a journey as a young adult. He desires to be on his own, but still needs the financial support of his parents. They hold a boundary by offering to subsidize him if he moves into a step down program while he attends college. The hero refuses the call, but the reality of not having enough resources to live on his own helps him decide to accept their proposal and agree to their conditions. He crosses the threshold to the special world *and moves into a college recovery program on the California coast. TJ learns the rules of the house and becomes acquainted with his roommates. He and his mentor, a young AA sponsor, attend meetings together and work through the twelve steps. There are trials to overcome on this new journey, such as having his bike stolen after forgetting to lock it, getting a ticket for not wearing a helmet, losing his wallet, and being caught at a party by campus police as a Minor in Possession (MIP) for holding a cup of beer. Slapped with an expensive fine for the MIP, he is summoned to court. He pays the fine with his hard-earned money.*

It is difficult at first for TJ to readjust to the rigors of being back in a mainstream school. But he eventually turns a corner and passes challenging computer science classes. To keep himself healthy and centered, he surfs, meditates, and practices deep breathing exercises.

Difficulties arise again when TJ abruptly leaves college life in 2020 because of the COVID-19 pandemic. He moves back home with his family. The journeyer does his best to use the regulation skills he'd learned in the wilderness to manage the feelings around being isolated and unsure about the future. But he faces his dragons and remains focused so he can someday graduate from college, work as an engineer in the sustainable energy field, and enjoy the fruits that life has to offer.

TJ's life journey remains to be continued ...

TJ's Final Reflections:

Saturday, 8/7/2021

Once I graduated aftercare, I still had not fully recovered or adopted a spiritual program in my life. I then went to college, where I moved into a sober living residence for students in recovery. There I met some of my closest friends who introduced me to Alcoholics Anonymous (AA). I went through the 12 steps, and that was what introduced me to my spiritual awakening. With the help of wilderness, aftercare, and my 12-step program, I was able to take steps to change how I live my life. Wilderness Therapy was the beginning of it all, and I can now thank my parents for giving me the chance to turn my life around.

HEROES OF MANY FACES

I felt pure joy that I've never experienced before; I felt the cleanest I've ever been, yet I was covered in dirt.

— Hunter
2019 Wilderness Therapy Graduate

Student Letters and Testimonials

The hero's journey is a circular passage traveled over and over, providing new opportunities to overcome and grow. TJ became one of the many heroes when he embarked on a wilderness journey. His dad and I were at first hesitant to separate him from the family. We were worried our precious child would feel cold, lonely, and abandoned and would never forgive us for sending him far away to the woods. Our fears came true, because he experienced all those things. But TJ persevered through the storms, climbed mountains, and faced his fears, like so many who preceded and traveled the road after him.

Wilderness Therapy is not only for teenage boys like our son, who suffered from depression, anxiety leading to weed addiction; this mode of therapy delivers positive outcomes for a wide range of behavioral and mental health challenges from preteen to young adults.

There are many outdoor therapy students whose lives have changed for the better from their wilderness journeys. Those successful ones typically apply the skills they learned in the woods to enjoy what the world has to offer, while generally preferring to keep their experiences private due to the stigma associated with mental health issues. For this chapter, a group of brave individuals have stepped up to contribute their stories of transformation by sharing their first and last wilderness letters and their concluding written testimonials. The letters show sentiments expressed when they first arrived at camp—refusing the call of getting the help that they needed—to the final letters, which show progress, strength, and healing. These heroes encompass both children and their families across various Wilderness Therapy programs, and their letters are published with their permission.

Carrin

Narrated by Carrin's Mother:

Backstory: Carrin was using alcohol and weed to self-medicate. She was also sneaking out and lying about it when questioned. Before she left for treatment, she was failing in school, stopped attending her classes entirely, and had suicidal thoughts.

Diagnosis: Generalized anxiety disorder, major depressive disorder, substance abuse, and suicidal ideation.

Types of Therapy Done at Home Prior to Wilderness Therapy: Traditional weekly therapy, antidepressants, six weeks at a residential treatment center (RTC), home for three weeks with psychiatric medications, therapy twice a week, AA meetings, and school supports.

Wilderness Therapy Program Attended: Open Sky

Age When Attended: Fifteen

Current Age: Twenty

Did You Hire a Transportation Service? I picked up Carrin myself from a local hospital after she was experiencing suicidal ideation, and we went straight to the airport. She knew she needed help and went willingly.

Did Your Child Go to Aftercare? Yes, Carrin went to therapeutic boarding school (TBS) for seven months after the wilderness program.

Do You Think Wilderness Therapy Made a Difference? Definitely. It was transformative for our whole family. Carrin still credits wilderness with saving her life.

Carrin's First Letter from Wilderness:

Monday, 2/12/18
Dear Mommy,
I miss you a lot. This isn't anything like you described to me. I'm dirty and cold and wet. I know that you and Dad think this is best, but I don't think you guys really know what we're doing because I'm so miserable, Mommy. I've been thinking a lot and don't think I was trying to the best of my abilities, and I wish that if you gave me the two weeks of me trying really hard not to be so miserable and I still don't think this place is right for me if you guys would let me come home and we could figure something else out.

Looking back, I wasn't trying hard enough to fight my depression and made a lot of mistakes in not putting all my effort into being open. I'm going to try with everything in me to make something positive out of these next two weeks, and if I still feel that this place is completely the wrong place for me to get better, I beg of you guys to let me get out of here and go someplace where I can focus on my feelings and emotions instead of being in the middle of the desert where I have to focus on making sure my fingers aren't falling off.

It's Monday, and we've yet to do any yoga or meditation. We wake up and pack up and hike, then eat lunch and set up where we're sleeping, then just hang out till dinner and sleep. I'm feeling like I'm always trying not to cry because I feel so alone.

I hope that your class is going well and that you're happy and that you know that I don't blame you or Dad for sending me here because you guys honestly thought this was the right thing for me, and you had no idea that this is as bad as it is. I don't know if this letter makes much sense because I'm crying, and my thoughts are jumbled, and I just wish that you could hold me.

I feel like you and Dad aren't going to listen to me, and even if I think this is wrong in two weeks, you're going to make me stay, but I beg of you to hear me out because if it's like this in two weeks, then this is not the environment for me to grow because I feel so unsafe out here. I love you a lot, and I hope you'll believe me and trust me when I say that wilderness is not the way for me to reach happiness. I feel that I learned everything I need to know at Polaris and that it's up to me to use that information. I'm sorry that I gave up, and that made you and Dad feel like this is what's best for me. But I'm not feeling guilty. I regret not trying the way I wish I did.

I love you so much, and I hope everything is well at home. I'm writing this on Tuesday the 12th, so on Tuesday the 26th (I think), I'll write again about this. I'll write you next week also, just not about whether or not this is best because from right now on I'm going to try not to get stuck in thinking about this.

I love you a lot, Mommy.

Love,
Carrin

Carrin's Final Letter from Wilderness:

Monday, 4/23/18
Dear Mommy,
Thank you for validating me, Mama. It feels good to be seen. I hear you feel encouraged when hearing my emotions regarding my dragon work. You feel this way because you believe I am growing in both strength and resilience. Your intention is to be open to learning about my dragons and supporting me in working with them. Your request of me is to open myself up and be vulnerable so I can dive into my work. I, too, am impressed with myself and the work I am putting in.

Thank you SO much for the pictures. I love them.

I'm keeping this letter short because we will be chatting on the phone, and I'm a busy gal this week.

OH! I went with two girls from my team and two guides on what's called a challenge hike. We hiked seven and a half miles on day one and ten on day two. It was hard, and afterward, I felt proud and believed I was extremely capable.

I love and miss you and will see you soonish. Here's a list of stuff I asked to pick up. Tons of black leggings without holes, exercise leggings, all spandex, all holey jeans I wear, jean shorts I wear, army green shorts, gray/brown university t-shirt, any/all big, soft, short sleeve t-shirts, long sleeve baseball tees with three buttons, any cute shirts—I trust you, normal socks—especially my silly ones, perfume ...

Much love,
Carrin

Carrin's Reflection on Her Wilderness Therapy Graduation:

Sunday, 7/11/2021
Blindfolded with outstretched arms, I was filled with an overwhelming mixture of both excitement and anxiety. I hadn't seen a familiar face in over twelve weeks, my only connection to the outside world being letters and the occasional phone call with my parents. Finally, my mom and stepdad, Peter, had made the trip to base camp to join me for a few days to immerse themselves in Wilderness Therapy. I felt my mom's presence before we reached each other. I recall being giddy to feel her touch again, wishing I could tear off the blindfold and run to her. And still, I remained mindful, making my way toward her, until at last, she was at my fingertips, and I collapsed into her arms. I was flooded with emotion: relief, longing, excitement, anxiety, and above all else, love. Too overwhelmed to say a word, I remained silent in her arms for what felt like forever, yet nowhere near long enough, knowing that she understood my lack of words.

We spent the next three days where the three of us had our own basecamp, a peaceful experience compared to life with the team of 8-12 other girls plus guides. With the help of our family therapist, each of us spoke our truth, sharing resentments, regrets, respects, and requests. We worked through tough, necessary conversations that continue to prove vital to our family dynamic to this day. We laughed, we cried, we ate unlimited cheesy tortes, and before I knew it, the time I had spent weeks wishing for and was now dreading quickly approached.

Before I departed from the Wilderness, the final moments consisted of my graduation ceremony with my team and my parents, as well as a ceremony with my fellow graduates. I felt a sense of camaraderie to the peers I was graduating with. Joy and love radiated throughout all of us as we completed this part of our journey and took our first steps into the unknown of the future.

Tyler

Narrated by Tyler's Mother:

Backstory: Tyler was unexpectedly cut from the basketball team in November of his sophomore year of high school. Shortly thereafter, he started having panic attacks at school, suffering from depression, losing weight, getting no exercise, and abusing substances. He started seeing an individual therapist. We also wanted him to see a psychiatrist, but he absolutely refused. I was terrified to let Tyler get his driver's license because he was so quick to anger and would get in such rages, I thought he would get behind the wheel and kill himself or somebody else. Then the shit hit the fan. Ty got arrested for criminal trespassing. Additionally, I found THC and vodka in his room, so we started drug testing. We attempted to begin family therapy but ended up sending Ty to wilderness before our family therapy appointment because things got too bad. We were afraid to leave Ty alone and his drug use increased.

Diagnosis: Depression, substance abuse, anxiety disorder.

Types of Therapy Done at Home Prior to Wilderness Therapy: We tried individual therapy. We took him to a psychiatrist, but he did not cooperate and ended up leaving the office cursing.

Wilderness Therapy Program Attended: Redcliff Ascent

Age When Attended: Sixteen

Current Age: Nineteen

Did You Hire a Transportation Service? Yes, as parents, we felt at ease after meeting the transport service that drove our son across the country. They met us at juvenile hall, and we told Tyler what was happening. They took him from there to Redcliff Ascent. We were told that he fought for the first two hours and beat on the glass so hard they were afraid he was going to break the window. They eventually stopped the car to restrain Tyler, and he tried to physically fight them. When head-butting one of the men, Tyler got a bloody nose. They sent me a picture and called me right away.

Did Your Child Go to Aftercare? Tyler went to a residential treatment center (RTC) for nine months after attending seventy-four days at Redcliff Ascent.

Do you Think Wilderness Therapy Made a Difference? We think Wilderness Therapy was a game-changer for Tyler. Change happened so much more quickly in wilderness than it did at the RTC. Tyler said wilderness helped him "see colors" again.

Tyler's First Letter from Wilderness:

Tuesday, 6/25/19
Mama,
Please get me out. It is too overwhelming. I can't do all this camping. They make you go out alone, and they build fires. Please, Mama, I'm scared and having an anxiety attack. Please get me out. I'm alone out here. Please, I'm begging. This isn't me! I have to leave, Mom. I'm getting desperate. I've tried to be strong, but I can't, please. I'm distraught, Mom. I'm begging you. You are my mother. I want to be with you. This is too much, Mom. All these people like the outdoors and making things. I'm stressed and the odd man out. I wake up multiple times every night and cry from homesickness. I'm not messing around. Please save me. I also want to hear you.

Same day. Two hours later.

Mama, please read the words. Please answer my panic. I have to see you. I can't stay out here. I've never been more stressed in my life. I need you. Please come get me. I can't be here another day. You don't know how much I miss you. I know you're probably listening to someone saying this is good for me, but Mama, I never felt panic like this. It's heartbreaking feeling alone like this. I can't even sit and cry alone because of the swarms of bugs. I know it sounds out of character for me to call you Mommy, but wow, I need you. I need a hug from you, Mommy.

I know this must be hard for you too. Can we end our suffering and see each other? When I'm home, we can do therapy together every day. Please hear me calling.

I wrote "Mama XOXO" on my hand to make me feel better today. I've been looking at it a lot. I'm swallowing my pride and saying I need you more now than I've ever needed anything in my life. I wrote a poem about you, but I can't send it cuz it wouldn't make sense without the right flow and rhythm. I know your intention wasn't to make me feel like this. That's why I'm stressing all of this to you. I'm not doing well because I feel helpless. The only person that can help me is across the U.S., but I can't call her. I need to be with you, Mama, more than you could ever know. I'm scared ...

XOXO

Love,
Tyler

Tyler's Final Letter from Wilderness:

Monday, 9/2/19
Dear Mama and Dad,
Guess what!? I got a knife! :) That is very, very rare out here! And I got selected to go to Dog Soldiers on Friday, which is also special! It is the leadership training, and only six people in all of RCA get to go. We got to make sandwiches, and we made a craft. I've come such a long way here. My staff was pleased. He was the one to knife me. My "intention" for the knife was to work as hard gaining your trust back as I did for the knife! So, you can hold me to that, Mama.

I love you and miss you. :) I'm phase complete as well. Now going for Fire Patch (one hundred fires). I'm pushing through this last however many days for you. The hard part about going to aftercare is not being with you both. I've worked hard and made so many changes, and it sucks not getting to live with you, but it's alright. In many months, when I'm out of aftercare, we can all be best friends again.

You'd be so proud of me. I'm a wildy expert now. I'm the leader of my group now, and I make the call on most of the decisions. I got named a couple of days ago too. My new name is Falcon of the Crow Moon. I have made a lot of improvement. I hope/think I'm leaving soon. I love you so much. Thank you for caring so much about my happiness.

Love,
Tyler
XOXO

Tyler's Personal Statement for College Applications:

Monday, 2/1/21
Coming to America, Tyler's Journey

Ten thousand feet up, looking off into the valley of the southern Utah desert, everything that had led me to this point, for a moment, did not matter. All I could do was smile, look around at my team and think, did we just climb this mountain?

Almost a year prior, I was cut from the varsity basketball team, which at the time encompassed much of my sense of belonging. Not having grown up in the U.S., I had always found my "family" and a connection to my American identity in my overseas basketball teams. The changed relationship with my teammates and new American community led me to question this foundation.

I began to experiment recklessly in an attempt to numb the unfamiliar, raw emotions I was feeling. Little did I know, what I was about to face would not only challenge my strength but my soul.

As a result of my behavior getting out of control, I was sent to a Wilderness Therapy program—colloquially referred to as "woods." Woods was unlike anything I could have imagined or anticipated. Some people might call it camping, but as I and my newfound companions would attest, it was hardly that. Our days consisted of hiking for miles and doing tasks out of our "phasebooks," a book of lessons and readings that guided us through the program.

Phasework put me in a position where I worked with others and asked for help, an area that needed improvement. Prior to this experience, asking for help felt like showing weakness. I learned that asking for help demonstrates humility and honesty. Executing phasebook tasks, such as making fire from sticks and stones, ultimately taught me a great deal about patience and perseverance.

As my peers and I turned our pain into passion, we let go of anger and motivated each other to act with optimism and positivity. The idea of turning pain into passion is a drive I apply to this day. I apply it to my growing business, putting time and persistence into my work even when I face obstacles or failures. After a few weeks in woods, I stopped keeping to myself; eating by the fire turned into my favorite part of the day and going to sleep meant cherishing life under the stars with my brothers.

Eventually, my direction and focus shifted to bettering myself and thriving in harsh conditions. This meant being passionate about my process instead of simply going through the motions. It meant working on my survival skills and on my relationships with my team. By processing and working through my setbacks, both individually and with my group, my communication skills improved drastically. When I returned to my budding business, I was able to recognize the importance of listening and understanding, much like I was able to in the Utah desert. I developed a belief that mindset turns into circumstance.

I transfer this skill of mindset creating reality into the endeavors I am currently pursuing. I now own and run a business I built from the ground up, online arbitrage sneaker flipping. I learn through my failures on a daily basis. I attribute this skill to the collection of my experiences in woods, laughing with my brothers in the midst of what seemed like our lives falling apart.

Scaling my business into what it is today is something I am very proud of, but truthfully, I believe I would be limiting myself by stopping here. I think to myself, how can I grow? What is my next mountain to climb? I believe pursuing higher education is the next step in my journey of success. Direction is something we depend on in life, and I am more than motivated and excited to shift my direction to bettering myself, my business and future business endeavors through pursuing higher education.

Katie

Narrated by Katie's Mother:

Backstory: Katie had been hospitalized five times, and her father and I had to think outside the box. Her diagnoses were all over the place at the time, as were her medications.

Diagnosis: Depression, anxiety disorder, learning disabilities in reading, ADHD, executive functioning deficits. She also suffers from trauma and PTSD.

Types of Therapy Done at Home Prior to Wilderness Therapy: Katie saw multiple psychiatrists and counselors. We also used Care Management Organization (CMO)–PerformCare, and we are currently using their services.

Wilderness Therapy Program Attended: Evoke Entrada

Age When Attended: Fourteen

Current Age: Sixteen

Did You Hire a Transportation Service? Yes, as heartbreaking as it was to have Katie picked up at the in-patient hospital, the transport service was flawless.

Did Your Child Go to Aftercare? Yes, Katie went to a residential treatment center (RTC) for thirteen months and then moved home when she graduated from the program.

Do You Think Wilderness Made a Difference? Evoke made a difference in my daughter's life and in my family's life. That was the first time that the true trauma unfolded, and it was not until then that we began to work on ourselves individually and together as a family. I am grateful for the ongoing supports provided by Evoke and for my parent mentor. We as a family have work to do, but we go at it differently and more authentically and honestly.

Katie's First Letter from Wilderness:

Wednesday, 9/18/19
Dear Dad,
I have been very strong out here, but I can't stop thinking of the last day I saw you, and I cry every time I think of that moment. I wanted you to know that I feel I was never allowed to cry at home and that I always had to be strong. I never felt as if my illness was seen or heard. I also did not feel well enough to share. I am very sick and very happy that I am getting the help that I need.

I am able to say everything about Pink Floyd and The Who. I impress people with my knowledge and feel like I'm under people my age and above them in ways they don't see. The adults see it, and that's no change. I think I need a higher amount of lithium or a new med. I have more paper, but that's all for poetry.

Otay Spanky

Later dude,
Katie

Katie's Final Letter from Wilderness:

Wednesday, 11/6/19
Hey Hey Hey Party People, (aka Mom and Dad)
I had a great week full of challenges and realizations. Some of those challenges being dealing with bipolar disorder. It is very hard, especially when being taken off mood stabilizers. Meaning, my brain randomly tells my body and brain to be sad. That sucks ass, but lately, I have been able to stay positive and motivated. This is a new skill—one that I am very proud of.

Hiking 24/7 isn't fun, but I hike alone so I can meditate on things that help me keep me centered. I have learned not to use my typical disconnect from everyone, and the lesson has served me well.

So, I just read Mom's letter. I sat and cried and then checked in with the group about how anxious and scared I am. I wish I could be with you, Mom; I love you so much. Spiritually I am holding your hand through this.

At the beginning of the week, it snowed, and it was fucking cold. In my perception, I think that lessons were taught and received.

I am very happy to get my aftercare letter because I am just so done with this outdoor shit in a bucket bullshit. I'm ready to enter a new stage of my life with open arms.

Love,
Kate

Katie's Wilderness Therapy Testimonial:

Sunday, 8/8/21
I went to Wilderness Therapy in August 2019 when I was fourteen. I was there for 13 weeks. Looking back, I think it helped me. It put my life more into perspective. You are stripped of the everyday clothing, makeup, and hairstyling. The dirt on your skin and in your hair is like a badge of honor, and nobody is judging. Taking away all beauty standards placed me in a situation where I felt safer than I was at home. I was able to break down rational skills with a lot of help and no judgment. I was able to take one moment at a time. My favorite part was singing on hikes and just being able to be me.

I am now 16, and I have been home for almost 8 months. I went back to my local public school and did okay academically. I am figuring out who I can trust with friendships. I am finding more self-worth every day. Even though living back home with my parents is going well, there is always work to be done. I plan to try to go to college, but right now, I am focusing on myself day to day.

Hunter

Narrated by Hunter's Mother:

Backstory: Hunter was self-harming, sneaking out in the middle of the night, drinking, and was refusing to go to school.

Diagnosis: Social anxiety disorder, depression.

Types of Therapy Done at Home Prior to Wilderness Therapy: Talk therapy, equine therapy, family therapy, Nexxus Therapy (targets to change neural pathways).

Wilderness Therapy Program Attended: Trails Carolina

Age When Attended: Thirteen

Current Age: Fifteen

Did You Hire a Transportation Service? We didn't use a transportation service. She knew a treatment program would be next if she acted out one more time. I told her three days before I took her. We drove, as it's three hours from our home.

Did Your Child Go to Aftercare? Yes, therapeutic boarding school for seven months.

Did Wilderness Therapy Help? Wilderness Therapy and aftercare made a huge difference and impact in Hunter's life. Nine months after she graduated TBS and before coming home, she went back to Trails to mentor for a week. She also wants to go back to the program again this summer to mentor. Wilderness Therapy not only changed Hunter, but it changed our family. We embraced all the tools she was learning, and while she was away, we started implementing them at home. Hunter has the self-awareness most adults don't have. She has the ability to see people, to see situations, and to see herself. She can recognize what is going on for her at any particular moment and make a course change. It might not always be immediately—she's a teenager. There are times she reacts rather than responds, but she will recognize it and come back to right the situation. The biggest change is that she wants to be a better person for herself, not because someone is forcing her to be better and not to be better for anyone else.

Hunter's First Letter from Wilderness:

Wednesday, 8/14/19
Hi Mom,
It's me, hehe, I'm alive (barely). I'm trying my best here, even though I'm really homesick and still getting comfortable with the group. I wanted to tell you that I am taking all accountability for my actions, such as when I would drink, juul, and sneak out. I want to say I made an agreement with myself that I am not ever going to do those things until I know how to be in control and am the appropriate age (not

including sneaking out because I'm never doing that again anyway).
I want you to know that you deserve a full explanation for all those
things. First up, juuling. I only did it because I wanted to be cool,
and to be honest, I only used it when I snapchatted it to people, and
this is embarrassing, but I didn't inhale it. I would just act like I was
to seem cool. Second up, drinking. I would only drink when I was
bored, and I know that's not healthy, but it's the truth. Sneaking out
is a big one.

As you know, me and Chad dated after you didn't give me the re-
sponse I needed. I felt abandoned, and this is how I coped. I would
get attached to one specific person and put all my needs, worries,
sadness, and anxiety on them. I would convince myself they were
helping me even though they weren't. So, I would be addicted to
them, and I would use them as my drug. It wasn't as unhealthy and
not OK, but it was all I had. I would do any certain thing to see him
or talk to him, not realizing how I was destructing the relationships
around me like you and my sisters. I am now self-aware and realize
it's not healthy and not something I am going to do anymore (or try
not to). That's also why I would steal my sister's electronics all the
time, so I could talk to him. I'd like to apologize for that.

Okay, so after I explained all that, I want to tell you before you sent
me here, I think I was doing good. My anxiety had gotten ten times
better; I was ready for school and put in all that effort. I was gonna
go to school, do my homework, go to cheer and stay organized.
I was so excited and ready to have a good year of not getting in
trouble, not doing bad things, being self-aware of my emotions and
how they are affecting the people around me. That was like my half-
way point. I was ready to have a good first day of school with all
my sisters, and then I got sent here. When I first got here, I was a
mess. Then I started opening up. Mom, I want to have a really good
relationship with you; I am ready for that. I've been ready for that
for a while (but I) didn't know how to start it. And it's my fault for
not opening up to you 'cause in the letter you wrote, I could tell you
were filling in blanks. I know I never talked to you about what's going
on with me and how I'm feeling. It's not because I don't want to. It's
just that I was a little scared of your response. I was so excited too
before I left, but I psyched myself out and didn't. And I am ready to
have a good relationship with my family. I think that I am mentally in
a good state.

I've been opening up so much here in the honor circle and to the other girls here. I also opened so much in my session with my therapist. We were talking about how I am ready to start relationships with you and the rest of the family and how I'm staying sober (not that I even like drinking or juuling cause it's disgusting). I do feel more self-confident each day when I wake up. I tell myself you are enough, you are worthy, you are beautiful, and don't let anyone tell you differently.

I think that I am personally in a good healthy mental state, and I am willing to help around the house and show some of the leadership skills I've learned here. I'll make dinner, organize your room, your second closet, or even clean the house like I did one time. OMG, I can teach you guys what FABs are. (Feeling About Because) — You state your Feeling (how) ... About (what) ... Because (why). It will help us all be aware of everyone's state of emotion, so we know how not to cross boundaries. Just ask me to do anything, and I'll do it without any follow-up questions. I think that I am in a good enough mental state to come home and have a fresh start, and so does my therapist. But it's up to you. Can you take this into consideration?

Also, this place freaking sucks. I had to strip naked in front of a girl I just met, take off all my jewelry (my earrings and dad's ring). I can't pee when I want or barely even shower. I've only showered once since I've been here. I can't sleep with my sloth or play with my ukulele. You have to eat all your food, and it's absolutely disgusting. I want to let you know my ear has gotten ten times worse, and it's giving me migraines. The Advil doesn't help. A bracket is still broken, it hurts really bad, and it's making me nauseous. And I'm on my period and have really bad cramps.

And oh, if you let me come home, I think I should go to a different therapist. You can sign me up for whatever music program or competition because I do have self-confidence about my singing, and I think I should pursue that talent.

Consider letting me leave cause I really am in a good mental state, and I'm ready to start over.

Love,
Huntie
(By the way, I smell disgusting)

Hunter's Final Letters from Wilderness:

Tuesday, 10/15/19
Dear Mom and Dad,
In my last letter, I was talking about taking accountabilities for all my past behaviors. I am now going to be telling you all the healthy intentions I have for the future. Before I do that, I want to say how sorry I am for the unhealthy actions and situations I had put myself in. I love you both so much. I am happy to see our family grow and learn from past experiences. In my LOA (Letter of Accountability), I talked about getting too attached to people, my low self-confidence, and my habits of isolating myself when I get stressed or overwhelmed. I could never face the truth and could never admit that these things were unhealthy and wrong. I am now aware of those things and am ready to move on and leave those actions in the past. From now on, I am going to recognize these behaviors when they are happening, so I am aware of them and am able to stop them before they get worse. I will openly communicate with my peers and with my family, so they know what's going on. I will stay away from alcohol and bad influences. I intend to keep my room and the house clean. I will do chores when I am asked, and I won't try to get out of it. I will keep myself present and not isolate myself. I will talk to my family whenever I am feeling stressed, anxious, or worried so we can go through it together.

When I am at home, I will face many challenges that might make it hard to stay on the healthy path. I will be put back into an environment full of bad influences, anxiety and go back to school. These things could cause me anxiety. And cause me to get attached to someone again or isolate myself. I am fully aware of these challenges and am ready to push through the temptations and stay on the path of no anxiety. I'm ready to open communication because I know how important these things are in my life. I intend to keep my body and mind a sacred place and will not tear it down but only build it up with encouragement and helpful and kind words.

These are things I am intending to do to put my path in the right, healthy direction. I am going to commit to the healthy coping and learning skills I learned here and incorporate them into my life in the real world. I love you both so very much and am excited to show both of you how much progress I've made. This letter I truly mean and am going to put full truth and effort into fulfilling it. I'm excited to see what the future holds for me and our family.

Love,
Huntie

Tuesday, 10/15/19
Hi Mom,
Your letter made me really happy reading that you forgive me, and you still love me. I am proud of myself for embracing this program and really accepted it! I'm excited to see you soon and tell you everything I've learned here! I miss you so much and love you a lot. I'm on phase 5!!! I'm almost phase six eligible too!!! :) Can you show my sisters my LOA (Letter of Accountability)? It would be nice for them to hear it.

In your last letter, I never got to answer your questions, so I'm going to do that now. For my TBS, could you maybe possibly go shopping for me and have Olivia pick out clothes? OK, so this is my list: From Pac Sun or somewhere else. Cute hoodies, white jean shorts, mom jeans, big T-shirts, Nike tank, sports bras, actual bras, underwear, cute tops, Birkenstocks, ukulele, make-up if I'm allowed, white Crocs ...

That's pretty much it. And for common ground, I have some ideas of what I want to do. See a movie, go bowling, shopping, get my hair done, go out to dinner, nails done, and get a massage. Those are all my advocacies. You're welcome!! Just so you have time to prepare, I'm really hoping I'm graduating on the 23rd, but I still don't know, and I'm scared that I'll have to stay here longer. I love you so so very much, and hopefully, I'm done with phase G in my next letter!!

Love Huntie (aka Stinky Butt)

Hunter's Wilderness Therapy Testimonial:

Tuesday, 9/21/21
Before I got sent to Wilderness Therapy, I was anxious, unappreciative, and lost. I didn't know what it meant to truly live. I was so consumed with the world I didn't even think that recognizing the things around me could fill the gap in my heart that I've known all

my life. When I first got there, I was in denial, and I didn't know what to expect. When I came to the conclusion that I needed help, that's when my life changed. I became so in touch with myself and the things and people around me. I was able to dig deep into my heart without the distractions of a normal life.

Yes, it was challenging and pushed me to the limits, but it shaped me into who I am today, and I will forever walk with this experience. Being in the woods I think was the most healing part. There's something special about the outdoors that seems to make the world's problems go away. I felt pure joy that I've never experienced before.

I felt the cleanest I've ever been, yet I was covered in dirt.

Light at the End of the Tunnel
by Hunter

There once comes a time all things have to pass
Even if it means they have to turn to ash
The darkness takes over
We forget about the light
The sun that shines down on the earth
To keep our days looking bright
So when the darkness begins to take over you
Look for the light at the end of the tunnel
Waiting to pull you through

AFTERWORD

A year after TJ completed his journey in the wilderness, I was helping him pack up to move to his college apartment. We came across artifacts from his time at the therapy program that had been kept in his file cabinet. There was the bow-drill set and his dirty canvas over-the-shoulder bag that never left his person during three months of expeditions. The bag was well worn and looks like a satchel Indiana Jones would carry. He let me take a peek so I could see the contents. When I lifted the flap, I found a folder with his letters, a student workbook, and his composition book. He allowed me to read a few passages of his journal. Soil was smudged all over the pages. His observations were incandescent, raw, and honest. It made me feel like I was right there with him. He always had such an extraordinary talent for expression.

Initially, I thought of putting the items in a keepsake box for him to open again someday, to remind him of the momentous time of his life that shaped him. But then I thought it would be such a shame for these vivid accounts to be locked away in a musty attic. I told him his letters and journals are treasures and should be put to light in a tale of triumph. I suggested he consider penning a book about Wilderness Therapy to help others understand what it was like to embark on such a voyage.

TJ agreed his story would make an interesting one and chuckled at the idea. As a movie buff, he took it further to say his adventure in the woods could even make an excellent film. However, he pronounced he did not have the energy or motivation to write anything like that himself. Then he pondered it some more and asked if *I* would write it for him. At first, I told him it was *his* story to write, not mine. But then I reminded myself that it *was* my story too. I also was part of this process, as a parent. TJ followed up by entrusting me with his writings. He encouraged me to take on the project.

When I was a preteen, my mom bought me a beautiful diary. I loved hiding away in my room so I could write about my feelings and log my daily dramas. I used to dream about becoming an author someday in the future. Although I thought the notion was ditched long ago, there I was in 2020 with this opportunity to write about something about which I truly feel passionate. I felt so honored and appreciated because my son trusted me to draft his story. And he gave me free rein to do so. Without any more hesitation, I took on the challenge.

TJ and I did not get started on this writing quest until he came home to live for summer break. He was nineteen years old at the time. We began one evening where we sat together on the couch, and he shared with me about the day he was transported to Utah. I recorded it with my iPhone. After this initial "interview," I gathered a list of questions that had been burning inside me but that I'd never thought to ask. I wondered how the block of cheese he was given as a personal food ration each week tasted after traveling inside his backpack for five or six days without refrigeration. (He said it did not taste sour.)

Between the recording sessions, I sifted through and organized selected letters and journal entries. TJ reminisced about events he never wrote to us about during his time in the program, which helped me fill in some of the gaps. Certain accounts seemed so ridiculous that we laughed together about them. For example, when he had to call out his name over and over when he went to the "bathroom," or the time when he had explosive "butt pee" in his sleeping bag in the middle of the night. One of the many things I love about TJ is his sense of humor, particularly about what must be a tough subject for him to recall. Some memories were extremely difficult for him to recount, as they brought his dragons back to life.

Drafting the manuscript was a hero's journey in itself. We began in the *ordinary world* at home, and I was called to adventure by being asked to author TJ's story. But then, one day during the course, I refused the call. This was when TJ told me he started having stressful dreams after our recording sessions. He was reliving his struggles from a detox-induced anxiety attack that occurred when he first arrived in Utah. The feeling of being stuck on a different planet came back to him. Suddenly he changed his tune about the project and shut down.

It was not my intention for this to be a negative experience for him, so I gave up on the idea altogether. I remember TJ's dad asking me, "Whatever happened to that book you were going to write?" I told him it was put to rest indefinitely.

Then one day, when I was participating in a support group meeting for families who were new to Wilderness Therapy, I was reinvigorated. What I noticed was that the *same* questions were being asked repeatedly by terrified and weary parents who were learning about the process. I thought of how helpful it would be for there to be a real story of a wilderness hero for people to read. Maybe then it wouldn't be so shocking for these parents or guardians to receive letters from their children who were begging to be rescued. Or if their child is recommended to transition to therapeutic boarding programs, the family will understand it's par for the course. Most importantly, that their kids need to maneuver through the freezing weather, the long and difficult hikes, and the hard and soft skills so they can eventually turn a corner that their families think they will never turn.

I believe it would be helpful for parents to understand that their children will struggle, but most will find their own way to get through it, and in doing so, they will feel so proud of their accomplishments. The labyrinth facing the families has now been traversed by many heroes before them, and that path is well known. What better way could there be than for the new families to read a book written by a veteran parent and son who have successfully conquered wilderness and the demons that took them there.

I realized this story would help others to recognize that, even though parents want to create a soft landing for their children and to prevent them from feeling cold, sad, desperate, and lonely, it does not help to rescue them. They need to rescue themselves. It is necessary for them to conquer the hardships so they can face their dragons head-on and return home with the reward of emotional resilience.

Once my son was in a better place in his life, I was able to reframe the project as a story meant to help other families. He liked this notion and encouraged me to continue the book. I accepted the challenge and crossed a threshold. In doing so, I met my mentors, who provided me with aids. The first one was my father, who authored three books and helped me edit all my first drafts. Then there was my son's wilderness therapist, who encouraged me with enthusiasm which fueled me to carry on, even when I wanted to give up. Other important mentors were my editors, who led me through the roadblocks with their wisdom and guidance.

The trials that faced me appeared as writer's block or a feeling of unworthiness in my abilities to find words to express my feelings. COVID-19 gave me more challenges because our whole family was home during the shutdown, and I could not find quiet places to work. At times I used this as an excuse, because I did not want to recall the difficult parts and avoided certain subjects. But I entered the inmost cave, faced my fears, and put this personal story out into the world.

This journey gave me the gift of enlightened parenting. There is still a lot to learn, and by no means am I an expert on this subject. Parenting takes a lot of patience and hard work. But I now have many useful aids to help me along the way, which are aids that I did not know existed only a few years ago.

I have my son, TJ, to thank for this creative opportunity in sharing our parallel process. He is such a special person who wears his heart on his sleeve and is not afraid to tell his story with all its warts. I love him, and I am incredibly proud. And through it all, I was finally able to do what was only a dream for me as a teenager: write a book about a subject I could not possibly love more.

Now I am ready to take on the next journey…

its gonna be ok,

Being a leader in the team is an awesome feeling

I've got the hard Skills down

I feel

my story. Its really sad and curious to see what that looks like coming from the other side of it. I get to give the boys some insight to what it is like when youve been here for as long as I have. It's really feels good when youre the one assuring people instead of people convincing you its gonna be ok.

Dear Mom & Dad,

In this letter, my goal is to take full responsib___ ___ ___ you guys in the past. I feel ___

for the wa___ ___ I've wronged the family
See and ti___ ___ wh___ what I've
one hope ___ with ___
done, ___
You und___
What ___
relati___ times ___

The time I felt like I was at my Best

Currently, I've been missing being close to my Parer___
its been a long time sense I have. It makes me really
song   thinking back on the ___ ___es I was closer ___
to them, I have some ___
kid, ___ting at ___ ___ries as a little
times I ___

I feel Statements
for Family

Dad
[I feel] Happy, hopeful, greatful

[When] I get to see you soon and I got to
talk to you about whats happening at home

[Belief] I value few___
has happened in you___

[Intention] Try___
off the weak s___

[Request] Ba___

[I feel]
On a___
So dea___

___ one of the ___
___ when I was for
San Clemente was
___ the beach ___
___ was
___ was ___ to
we ___
___ we're my
the ___

Ceremony for mom

Reason for ceremony
• Connection with mom is a very disconnect
• Want to hit restart button on relationship
• Music of solitude represents how my connection
  with my mom was (not sharing emotions, isolation,
  frustration that I cant connect)

What this ceremony will be
• Break the disconnect
• Tomorrow morning (after Music of Solitude day)
  the team will be woken up by the guides and
  be brought toward me sight
• I'll be sitting in a circle

Mask of Solitude

Morning

I
is
these

this day of
how the teams
leading this morning

Team c

meal

upset

much

Pizza

Sauce - • Cut onion into 1/3 and dice into
            pieces
• Salt
• Pepper
• Itow
• 1/2 of bucket full of water
• oil
• ???
• little bit of Hot Sauce
• + Pow (lots of it)

Dough

I'd like very much to go ... Bonus
her and tell her how I feel, even throwing power
I'll be away for so long.

Solo Dinner (Done)

Ingredients	Directions
• Pasta	Cook th cut on the fire
• Bell peppers	until ready
• Kale	• add salt & oil
• ??? onions	
• Green beans	

drop

camp but not ha

MY RESEARCH

Educational Consultants

Educational consultants, known as ECs, have working insider knowledge of therapeutic treatment programs. By networking and traveling to visit facilities, they learn about the directors, the therapists, and the current population of students. While conventional therapists and counselors sometimes have had a client attend a wilderness or other treatment program, they likely have not visited and are not aware of the range of alternatives. That is what an EC specializes in.

Competent ECs help raise the chance of a treatment experience's success by minimizing trial and error that comes with mental health issues and help to stay clear of potential treatment failures by avoiding the pitfalls of unethical treatment programs. Such efficacy information is something parents and caregivers simply do not have access to, no matter how much research is done, especially during a time of crisis.

The cost of hiring an EC seems exorbitant, especially since it's not often covered by insurance, but I found it to be worth every penny in the long run. The fee usually includes as many placements as needed, weekly updates with the therapists, advocating for their clients, and their general expertise.

Not all ECs are created equal, however, and the best way to find one is through a referral from a parent, therapist, or through independent associations such as the IECA (Independent Educational Consultant Association) and TCA (Therapeutic Consulting Association). It is important the EC has an independent status, which means they remain a neutral party and never receive compensation for a placement in any program.

Why Wilderness Therapy Is Powerful

Before enrolling my son in a Wilderness Therapy program, I did not understand how spending three months in the woods related to real-world experiences. I would ask, "How would busting a fire without matches be useful, unless there was a future apocalypse?" I subsequently found an incredible wealth of information on Dr. Will White's podcast, *Stories from the Field: Demystifying Wilderness Therapy*. Featured on the show are a broad range of guests who are involved in the field of Outdoor Behavioral Healthcare. Dr. White is also the author of the book *Stories from the Field: A History of Wilderness Therapy*.

I was intrigued by listening to podcast episode #130 with Dr. Mike Gass, who serves as director of the Outdoor Behavioral Healthcare Center and the NATSAP Research Database Network. During the show, he discussed his current project studying the effectiveness of Adventure Therapy at the University of New Hampshire, which is being funded by a $3 million grant. He has written a multitude of journal articles on topics such as risk management, safety, and cost-benefit analyses. I contacted him with questions about his research. He allowed me to share an acronym he uses to help describe how and why Adventure Therapy is effective called "SUBMARINES":

SUBMARINES

S = saturated environment/participants experience adventure therapy 24/7

U = unique physical environment/unique social environment

B = body health: good food, good sleep, good exercise

M = metaphor

A = action orientation

R = real consequences

I = intentionality of program

N = nature

E = eustress (the positive use of stress)

S = solution orientation

Beneficial for Mental and Physical Health

It is a well-known fact that being outdoors is good for mental and physical health. I was fascinated to read in Dr. White's book *Stories from the Field* about a time in 1901 when the Manhattan State Hospital "insane asylum" separated tuberculosis-infected patients from the non-infected patients by placing them in outside tents. Significant improvements were discovered in the general well-being of the patients in tents compared to the ones who stayed indoors. It eventually resulted in the discharging of many patients who had recovered from the disease. Following this finding, "Tent Treatment" became a widespread form of therapy at hospital facilities throughout the country.

Researchers of Outdoor Behavioral Therapy have demonstrated that, in addition to professional counseling, fresh air, exercise, regular sleep, and good nutrition significantly improves the health of their students. In one selective study published by Steven DeMille and Anita Tucker, it was found that adolescents who were overweight lost weight, while underweight adolescents gained muscle weight. Additionally, those who were normal weight lost fat and gained muscle mass.

Incorporates Metaphoric Transfer

A journal article written by Dr. Gass, called *Enhancing Metaphor Development in Adventure Therapy Programs* (1991), highlighted how outcomes from outdoor therapy are pronouncedly improved when the program associates the field experiences metaphorically with home life challenges. The linking of insights and skills from one environment to the next is a parallel process. This study by Dr. Gass has shown that these explicit parallels improve students' emotional preparedness for the return home.

Serves as a Stabilizer

Most struggling adolescents and young adults receive professional recommendations to begin their treatment journey in a wilderness program instead of going straight to a residential treatment center (RTC). The reason for this, as specified by my educational consultant Teri Solochek, is that "It enables the therapeutic team to see what the child looks like away from home and the stressors and influences of peers, family, substances, school, technology, and so on. A wilderness program serves as both a stabilizer and an assessment." Dr. Solochek also stated that the wilderness setting provides a realistic picture of the student such that they do not become over-pathologized, and there is a clearer idea of the root causes of their behaviors. In her experience, she finds it often leads to a lesser, and less expensive, level of care than going directly to an RTC. It can also mean the child can transition home after a wilderness program with positive community supports. Significantly more progress can be made in ten to twelve weeks of outdoor therapy than in the first few months of a therapeutic boarding program. It is important to point out that there are times when an OBH program might not be appropriate, which is why a professional consultant may be particularly helpful.

Many parents in my Wilderness Therapy support group felt like they were thrown a curveball when their therapeutic team recommended that their child transition into long-term residential treatment after the completion of their wilderness program. However, Wilderness Therapy is considered the catalyst, or short-term intervention. The typical stay, which on average is about three months, is not long enough to solidify changes. Studies have shown that there is a better chance of success if the student moves on to treatment at an aftercare program. (According to Dr. Gass, about 50 percent of adolescents who complete Adventure Therapy programs transition to aftercare, and about 50 percent take the road home.)

The Common Path of Treatment chart, on the following page, gives a general idea of treatment scenarios, with the number one goal being stabilization.

Changes the Mindset

Another reason for launching the treatment path in a Wilderness Therapy program is that it creates a change of mindset before a child continues with longer-term care. According to a model of behavior change called the Transtheoretical Model, or Stages of Change, there are six stages individuals go through to change a behavior. Stage One, called *pre-contemplation*, is when a struggling teen first arrives at their outdoor therapy program. They feel their mothers and fathers are being unreasonable, and they have no

COMMON PATH OF TREATMENT:
THE LONG AND SHORT ROAD

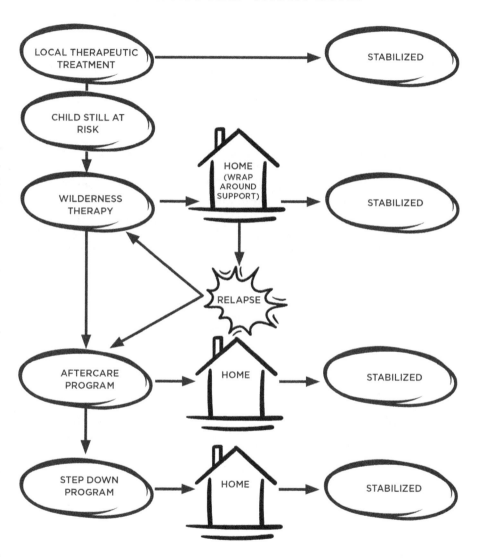

Flow chart was adapted from a diagram found in the book *What Now? How Teen Therapeutic Programs Could Save Your Troubled Child* (2007) by Dr. Paul Case.

intentions of making a change. While progressing through the course of the program, they merge into Stage Two, or the *contemplative stage*. In this stage they begin to take ownership of their negative behavior. Once the students transition to aftercare, they are in a better headspace and are more apt to continue with the next four steps: *preparation, action, maintenance,* and *relapse. (See Chapter Twelve page 132 to view the Transtheoretical Model diagram)*.

Additional Wilderness Therapy Studies

Wilderness Therapy Is Relatively Safe

According to a ten-year study conducted by Dr. Gass's research team, children are safer in wilderness programs than at home. It was found that the average American adolescent was two times more likely to visit an emergency room than an OBH Council program participant. The injury rate for Wilderness Therapy participants is 1.12 per 1,000 students. For comparison, there are 19.74 injuries per 1,000 from football practice and 3.28 per 1,000 from downhill skiing.

Wilderness programs that are accredited by AEE–OBH, an independent credentialing body for OBHC programs, are held to a high set of standards, ethics, and risk management. They are not unregulated, punitive, or militaristic teen boot camps reminiscent of the 1980s and '90s. These facilities must abide by established best practices for safety and treatment. Wilderness Therapy programs today bear little resemblance to the "tough love" approaches of programs from decades long past.

With any kind of program in the outdoors, there will be a reasonable number of risks, especially for teenagers challenged with mental health issues, behavioral issues, or substance abuse. It is simply not possible for the program directors to guarantee total protection from incidents or injuries. On the other hand, being in the wilderness means there is no access to drugs, vape shops, tall buildings, razors, friends who drive drunk, and online predators.

Wilderness Therapy Is Costly, Yet Cost-Effective

Wilderness Therapy comes with a hefty price tag and is not typically covered by insurance. The daily rate is equivalent to a night at the Four Seasons—for your child to sleep on the ground under a tarp! With added enrollment fees and transportation expenses, the cost may be unfortunately out of reach for the average family. Even though individual and group therapy can be reimbursed, and insurance advocates may be of help in recovering expenses, most families still need to dig deep in their pockets to pay the remainder of the bill. Some individuals take out home loans, borrow from their 401(k), or use college savings to help with the costs. There are also several scholarships available for those who qualify. (*See* Resources *for a list of methods to assist with the cost of Outdoor Behavioral Therapy.*)

Although Outdoor Behavioral Healthcare seems pricey, the latest study conducted by the University of New Hampshire involving teens with dual diagnosis has proven that it's two times less expensive and more effective than traditional forms of therapeutic treatments. One of the purposes of the analysis, which was published in the journal *Substance Abuse: Research and Treatment*, was to offer evidence to insurance companies showing this treatment is not only effective but could prevent multiple trips to the emergency room or drug rehabilitation centers. Additionally, completion rates were found to be 94 percent for Outdoor Behavioral Healthcare, compared to all other therapies.

GLOSSARY

Alcoholics Anonymous (AA): An international fellowship of individuals who have had a drinking problem. It is nonprofessional, self-supporting, multiracial, apolitical, and available everywhere. There are no age or education requirements. Membership is open to anyone who wants to do something about their drinking problem. *https://www.aa.org*

Aftercare: A continuum of care post-wilderness to help cement or reinforce the new skills learned in treatment. It usually refers to therapeutic boarding schools (TBS) and residential treatment centers (RTC) but can also include intensive outpatient programs (IOP) or wrap-around services.

Approach to the inmost cave: This stage is described as a dark and scary place where the treasure of emotional resilience resides.

Atonement: When the hero is reborn and in harmony with life and the world. The imbalance that sent this person on the journey has been amended.

Bow drill: Tool to make fire. Wilderness Therapy students learn how to make bows by carving tree branches and tying rope at both ends to make a bow.

Busting a coal: A primitive technique to make fires by rubbing sticks together to create enough friction to produce a burning ember.

Call to adventure: The first stage of the journey, in which the hero has been summoned.

Cannabis: A group of three plants with psychoactive properties: Cannabis *sativa*, Cannabis *indica*, and Cannabis *ruderalis*. The dried flowers of these plants are ingested or inhaled for their psychoactive properties and commonly known as weed, pot, or marijuana.

Cognitive Behavior Therapy (CBT): Psychotherapy that deals with a range of mental illnesses while focusing on emotion regulation, behavior modification, and development of personal coping strategies to aid in solving current problems. It is considered a "solutions-oriented" form of talk therapy.

C-pack (construction pack): Hand-constructed backpack made by rolling up belongings in a tarp and tying them all together with rope. In many outdoor therapy programs, a C-pack is the initial backpack used before earning a real camping backpack. It is a teaching tool because it takes patience and time to pack properly. If not done right, it can sit uncomfortably on the back or fall apart during expeditions.

Crossing the threshold: The hero is finally committed to the journey by crossing a threshold into the *special world*, where trials and adventure await.

Dialectical Behavior Therapy (DBT): A specific type of psychotherapy developed by psychologist Marsha M. Linehan. Teaches skills to manage painful emotions and decrease conflict in relationships. The four key areas DBT focuses on are mindfulness, distress tolerance, emotion regulation, and interpersonal effectiveness.

Educational consultant (EC): Independent consultant who helps find placements in therapeutic programs for children struggling with mental health. Programs include Outdoor Behavioral Healthcare, residential treatment centers (RTCs), therapeutic boarding schools (TBSs), intensive outpatient programs (IOPs), recovery programs, or young adult transition programs. They also can assist with psychological testing and special education advocacy.

Face the dragons: A psychological metaphor for overcoming and facing obstacles, despite one's fears.

Family systems approach: A therapeutic approach wherein the family members work together to identify and achieve goals. Studies show that Outdoor Behavioral Healthcare programs that use the family systems approach have better outcomes than those that do not.

Feelings Wheel: A wheel illustration created by Dr. Gloria Willcox, made up of descriptive emotion words to help identify what you are feeling.

Field guides: Members of the treatment team who keep students safe on their expeditions with round-the-clock supervision. They manage group processing and therapy assignments, plan ceremonies, and give feedback to the therapist. These important mentors also teach the students how to stay warm, make shelter, bust coals, and cook meals.

Fire board: Part of a bow drill set made of a flat piece of wood where the spindle rests as it spins to create friction to bust a coal.

Fire vigil: A period of wakefulness while keeping a fire burning. In Wilderness Therapy, students stay up all night tending to the fire. It usually occurs during solos and group bonding events.

Five stages of grief: According to psychiatrist Elisabeth Kübler-Ross, there are the five stages people go through when experiencing grief: denial, anger, bargaining, depression, and acceptance.

Four Corners: Where the borders of Colorado, Utah, Arizona, and New Mexico touch.

GeneSight genetic testing: Test using saliva sample to analyze how genetics may affect the outcomes of psychiatric medications.

Hero: The protagonist on a journey.

Hero's journey: A heroic character sets out on a journey, has transformative adventures, and makes a triumphant return home. It is a basic repeating pattern found in many stories from around the world throughout history and was coined by Joseph Campbell, who authored the book *The Hero with a Thousand Faces.*

Hero's return: The hero completes the adventure and brings home special knowledge as a result of going full-circle on the journey.

Home contract: A written contract between parents or guardians and their children, to provide boundaries that integrate rules, values, and expectations of improved behaviors. Frequently used with a teen or young adult transitioning from the structure of residential treatment to the structure of their home.

***I-feel* statement:** An effective communication tool used to help clarify emotions and beliefs. It helps the listener to better understand the speaker's emotions.

Impact letter: A therapeutic tool used to explain why you think your child needs to be in treatment, in hopes your child gains perspective on their life and how they affected others around them.

Individualized Education Program (IEP): A written legal document developed with a team of teachers and administrators for public school children who are eligible for special education services. The purpose is to help kids who need extra support to thrive in school. Accommodations can include extended time on tests, study skills classes, speech-language therapy, and assistive technology. A 504 plan is similar and acts as a blueprint for how the school will support a student with a disability and remove barriers to learning.

Intensive outpatient program (IOP): A kind of treatment service and support program that integrates treatment into a patient's daily routine. Program hours could be after school or after work for 4–5 hours a day, where patients undergo individual and group therapy.

Juniper tree: Coniferous tree or shrub in the cypress family. A common species of trees in the Utah desert.

Master of two worlds: The hero has gone full-circle through the monomyth by traveling from the *ordinary world* to the *special world* and back to the *ordinary world* again. He/she/they have experienced and gained an understanding of both worlds.

Mentee: The student who needs to absorb the mentor's knowledge and have the ambition and desire to know what to do with this knowledge.

Mentor: An experienced and trusted adviser. Wilderness Therapy mentors come in the form of the primary therapist, field guides, and students who are further along in the program.

Metaphoric transfer: The linking of insights and skills achieved from one learning environment (Adventure Therapy program) to another (home life) and how these skills apply to future situations.

Mindfulness: The practice of paying attention to the present moment and doing so intentionally and with non-judgment.

Monomyth: A cyclical journey in which a heroic protagonist sets out, has transformative adventures, and returns home. This is a basic repeating pattern found in many stories from around the world throughout history. The term was coined by philosopher Joseph Campbell, who wrote the book *The Hero with a Thousand Faces.*

Mormon tea: Leafless evergreen shrub commonly found around the outdoor therapy campsites in the Four Corners region. Presents with bright green, wiry stems. It is said to have been used by Mormon pioneers to make medicinal tea.

Nest: Kindling created with pine needles, shredded tree bark, or dry grass, used to spark a flame when active coal dust is tapped into the center and oxygen is blown into it.

Ninety days of darkness: The three months it takes to adjust to life after Wilderness Therapy. This is when there is the highest risk for relapse. After graduation from the outdoor program, there is this "mountaintop experience," often followed by a period of emotional downturn.

Neuropsychological testing: Evaluations administered by trained professionals which include written, visual, or oral tests to assess neurological and emotional functioning. Provides an additional layer of assessment for the therapist and aids the treatment team in making aftercare decisions.

Ordeal: When the hero faces his dragons and discovers an enlightened version of himself. This stage symbolizes a death and rebirth.

Ordinary world: The beginning of the story where we see the hero's normal life before the adventure begins.

Parallel process: It is a family systems approach to therapy when a child is in a residential treatment setting. The family works on similar therapeutic assignments, communicates through letters, practices similar self-care routines alongside their child from afar. The goal is to learn healthier communication skills and coping mechanisms to foster strong familial bonds when it comes time to reconnect.

Partial hospitalization program (PHP): Program to treat mental illness and substance abuse. Patient continues to live at home but goes to the treatment center daily. More demanding than the IOP treatment.

Psychiatrist: A doctor who specializes in prescribing mood-altering medications. Most Outdoor Behavioral Healthcare programs partner with psychiatrists to aid students who need medication management while they are enrolled.

Reactive parenting: When parents or caregivers act on their own emotions in response to a child's behavior instead of being mindful.

Reflective listening: When the listener repeats what the speaker said, which results in the speaker feeling heard. It helps to clarify emotions.

Refusal of the call: The hero refuses the journey at first because he has deep personal doubts about leaving the comfort of his home to face challenges in an unknown world.

Residential treatment center (RTC): Longer-term therapeutic programs described as behavioral and emotional support, addressing physical, emotional, behavioral, familial, social, and intellectual/academic development.

Road of trials: The hero endures tests and trials in the *special world*, which are an important part of the journey for emotional growth.

Road to aftercare: The phase in which the hero can see hope and is close to finishing the journey towards home, but not before he must face more tests and challenges at an aftercare program.

Sagebrush: A perennial shrub found in the desert, commonly used for smudging ceremonies.

Seizing the treasure: The stage of the hero's journey in which the hero has overcome the trials and earns a reward.

Self-care: The act of caring for one's needs to be able to take care of others.

SIFT technique: A four-step strategy from Dan Siegel, MD, used to slow our brain down and connect with what we are feeling. SIFT stands for sensations, images, feelings, thoughts.

Smudging ceremony: Ceremonies using aromatic smoldering sage bundles. A widespread practice among Indigenous peoples of the Americas.

Socket: Part of a bow drill set. It is usually a piece of rock with a depression where the spindle is held in place vertically as it spins between the socket and fireboard.

Solo: An outdoor task in which wilderness students spend time alone in silence, allowing them to reflect on themselves and their past choices and find their inner strengths.

Special world: The unfamiliar place where the action of the story takes place. The hero leaves the comfort of home, crosses the threshold, and enters a *special world* full of challenges and rewards.

Spindle: Part of a bow drill set. A long and rounded piece of wood with a pointy tip that spins into the fireboard to create friction hot enough to bust a coal.

Spoon: Utensil carved from a tree branch to eat with while on the wilderness journey. Typically, programs require the students to whittle them as a teaching tool.

Stages of change: (Also called Transtheoretical Model) Stages a person goes through when trying to change a behavior such as substance abuse, eating disorders, or gaming addictions, to name a few. Individuals move through six stages of change: pre-contemplation, contemplation, preparation, action, maintenance, and termination. Model developed by Prochaska and DiClemente.

Step down program/Transitional living: Final phase of treatment for graduates of primary treatment programs. Allows them to continue building a better foundation as they live more independently.

Supernatural aids: Tools to help the hero on the journey such as mentors, letters, bow drills, and new communication skills.

THC: Tetrahydrocannabinol, the chemical responsible for most of marijuana's psychological effects. It acts much like the cannabinoid chemicals made naturally by the body, according to the National Institute on Drug Abuse (NIDA).

Therapeutic boarding school (TBS): Longer-term therapeutic program that includes therapeutic and academic aspects addressing physical, emotional, behavioral, familial, social, and intellectual/academic development.

Three-part breath: A breathing exercise using three parts of your body: the lower belly, mid-chest, and upper chest. It works by filling your lungs with air and directing the oxygen toward each section three times as you exhale completely.

Transitional living/Step down program: Final phase of treatment for graduates of primary treatment programs. Allows them to continue building a better foundation as they live more independently.

Transtheoretical model: *See* Stages of Change, page 132.

Transport service: Professional crisis intervention service that escorts students to their outdoor therapy programs, residential treatment centers, or therapeutic boarding schools in a safe manner. They are experts in deescalating high-running emotions.

Validation: The act of noticing what is being felt by someone else and then showing an understanding of where the person is coming from.

Vaping: The inhaling of a vapor created by a battery-powered electronic cigarette (e-cigarette). Flavored nicotine and other chemicals are delivered through cartridges filled with liquid that are heated into a vapor. Popular among teens because they are shaped like a USB flash drive, which makes them easy to hide from parents and teachers. The nicotine in one vape cartridge is equal to that of 20 cigarettes. Cartridges can be replaced with THC (the psychoactive chemical found in marijuana).

Wax/cannabis wax/Weed wax: An extremely potent form of marijuana concentrate that has a consistency of yellow, gooey wax.

Weed: *See* Cannabis

Wilderness therapist: The key mentor who meets with the wilderness student in the field for individual and group therapy. They coordinate the treatment team consisting of field guides, psychiatrists, and psychological test evaluators and communicate with the families and educational consultants.

Wilderness Therapy: An experiential form of mental health treatment for struggling adolescents and young adults that combines outdoor experiences with individual and group therapy.

RESOURCES

RECOMMENDED BOOKS

Advice for Parents

Case, Paul. *What Now?: How Teen Therapeutic Programs Could Save Your Troubled Child*. Franklin, TN: Common Thread Media, 2007.

Jimenez, Ruben. *The Road Home: A Guide for Parents with Teens or Young Adults Returning from Treatment*. Ojai, CA: Road Books, 2014.

Pozatek, Krissy. *The Parallel Process: Growing Alongside Your Adolescent or Young Adult Child in Treatment*. Brooklyn, NY: Lantern Books, 2011.

Reedy, Brad M. *The Journey of the Heroic Parent: Your Child's Struggle & the Road Home*. New York: Regan Arts, 2015.

Thayne, Tim R. *Not by Chance: How Parents Boost Their Teen's Success in and After Treatment*. Charleston, SC: Advantage Media Group, 2013.

Wilderness Therapy Insights, Research, and History

Ferguson, Gary. *Shouting at the Sky: Troubled Teens and the Promise of the Wild*. Helena, MT: Sweetgrass Books, 2009.

Gass, Michael A., H.L. "Lee" Gillis, & Keith C. Russell. *Adventure Therapy: Theory Research and Practice*. New York: Routledge, 2011.

Hunt, John F. *Walking with Jason*. Bloomington, IN: AuthorHouse, 2013.

White, Will. *Stories from the Field: A History of Wilderness Therapy*. Jackson, NH: Wilderness, 2015.

RECOMMENDED PODCASTS

Finding You: An Evoke Therapy Podcast
Host: Dr. Brad Reedy
https://podcasts.apple.com/us/podcast/finding-you-an-evoke-therapy-podcast/id1157223571

Hopestream for Parenting Kids Through Drug Use and Addiction
Host: Brenda Zane
https://podcasts.apple.com/us/podcast/hopestream-for-parenting-kids-through-drug-use-and/id1494533993

In the Trenches
Host: Andrew Taylor
https://podcasts.apple.com/us/podcast/in-the-trenches-podcast/id1313522266

SKYlights
Host: Open Sky Wilderness Therapy
https://podcasts.apple.com/us/podcast/id1463239577

Stories from the Field: Demystifying Wilderness Therapy
Host: Dr. Will White
https://podcasts.apple.com/us/podcast/stories-from-the-field-demystifying-wilderness-therapy/id1440862416

Wilderness Therapy & Residential Treatment Center Journey
Host: Andy Goldstrom
https://podcasts.apple.com/us/podcast/wilderness-therapy-residential-treatment-center-journey/id1508380762

ASSISTANCE WITH FINDING THERAPEUTIC PROGRAMS

All Kinds of Therapy
A website with a comprehensive, independent fact-based online directory for Family Choice Behavioral Healthcare Interventions (FCBHI) and the substance abuse industry for troubled teens and young adults.

Web: *https://www.allkindsoftherapy.com*

IECA: Independent Educational Consultants Association
The Independent Educational Consultants Association (IECA) is a not-for-profit, international professional association representing experienced independent educational consultants.

Web: *https://www.iecaonline.com*

TCA: Therapeutic Consulting Association
Professional association for therapeutic consultants and other referring professionals, dedicated to advancing the field of therapeutic consulting through collaboration, training and education, outcome-based research, support of ethical standards, and an ongoing review of best practices.

Web: *https://www.therapeuticconsulting.org*

TESTIMONIALS

Thriving Now Movement
A website, maintained and moderated by a parent of a child who attended residential therapeutic programs, to shed light on the positive stories of Wilderness Therapy and residential treatment.

Web: *https://www.thrivingnow.me*

OUTDOOR BEHAVIORAL HEALTHCARE TRADE ORGANIZATIONS

AEE: Association for Experiential Education

Association to elevate and expand the global capacity of experiential education by building an inclusive and accessible community for experiential education professionals who are firmly rooted in the philosophy, principles, and practices of experiential education. They support the academic research, publication, and dissemination of authoritative information for promoting, implementing, and advancing the philosophy, principles, and practices of experiential education.

Web: *https://www.aee.org*

NATSAP: National Association of Therapeutic Schools and Programs

Organization of therapeutic schools, residential treatment programs, wilderness programs, outdoor therapeutic programs, young adult programs, and home-based residential programs for adolescents and young adults with emotional and behavioral difficulties. It serves as an advocate and resource for information about members of their organization. Ensures that the industry provides the highest quality services to the young people and families they serve.

Web: *https://www.natsap.org*

OBH Council: Outdoor Behavioral Healthcare Council

A voluntary credentialing program for Outdoor Behavioral Healthcare (OBH) providers. Provides impartial validation that the program meets or exceeds standards that have been developed exclusively for OBH programs. Accredited programs must demonstrate that they operate above industry standards of ethical care, treatment evaluation, and risk-management practices, and have solid evidence of a program's commitment to quality and adherence to professional standards.

Web: *https://obhcouncil.com*

METHODS OF ASSISTANCE TO HELP
WITH THE COST OF WILDERNESS THERAPY

Scholarships

Choose Mental Health
Mission: To empower families around mental health needs. This includes educational and financial support. Families qualify for a scholarship based on hardship. The family needs must fit within the network of providers' treatment ability. These providers are committed to a higher level of care that benefits the family. To begin the process, visit the website. Each request is based on fit and available funding. Restrictions apply.

Web: *https://choosementalhealth.org*

Evoke Family Foundation
Mission: To increase access to and awareness of Evoke Wilderness Therapy by engaging a broader and more diverse community through outreach activities and financial support to families who would otherwise not have the means to send their loved ones to the program.

Email: *director@evokefamilyfoundation.org*
Web: *https://evokefamilyfoundation.org*

Jason William Hunt Foundation
Mission: Supports families in crisis through therapeutic wilderness expedition treatment programs. Each of the treatment providers they work with match the award money they receive. Visit the website for a list of treatment providers and application procedures.

Email: *John@jwhf.org*
Web: *https://www.jwhf.org*

LOA Fund
Mission: Supports qualified individuals who would benefit from Outdoor Behavioral Healthcare treatment for mental health or addiction, including education, prevention, and treatment.

Email: *loafund@gmail.com*
Web: *https://www.samhsa.gov/grants*

Parker Bounds Johnson Foundation
Mission: Supports Oregon and Washington resident adolescents and young adults in need of wilderness treatment.

Email: *info@pbjwilderness4life.org*
Web: *https://pbjf.org*

Saving Teens in Crisis Collaborative (Saving Teens)
Mission: Supports families with struggling adolescents needing therapeutic programs and schools but without financial ability.

Email: *kbrown@savingteens.org*
Web: *http://savingteens.org*

Sky's the Limit Fund
Mission: To transform the lives of youth in crisis and their families by providing access to Wilderness Therapy programs, coaching services to guide families during the transition home, and outreach to educate the community on the benefits of Wilderness Therapy. Supports youth and young adults in crisis, ages 11–25, for families with financial needs.

Email: *info@stlfgives.org*
Web: *www.skysthelimitfund.org*

Other

Health Insurance
Most Outdoor Behavioral Healthcare programs are not covered by insurance; however, some may cover a portion of the group and individual therapy.

Health Insurance Advocates
Working with an insurance advocate can improve chances of recovering a percentage of cost through reimbursement after the fact. Engage them early

in the process for best results. Below are several companies to contact if you choose this route:

Alpha Billing
Web: *https://www.alphamedbilling.com*

Bridgeway Billing
Web: *https://www.bridgewaybilling.net*

Denials Management
Web: *https://fixmyclaim.com*

Mental Health and Autism Project
Web: *https://www.mhautism.org*

SJ Health Insurance Advocates
Web: *https://www.sjhealthinsuranceadvocates.com*

Medical Care Deduction
The Internal Revenue Code allows a deduction for medical care of the taxpayer, the taxpayer's spouse, or dependents if those expenses exceed 10 percent of the taxpayer's adjusted gross income. Deduction approvals will depend on why your child was placed in a therapeutic boarding school. Alcohol and substance abuse placements are tax deductible, as well as some placements for learning disabilities.

Federal Mental Health Parity Law
This law states that health plans which offer mental health benefits MUST offer them in parity with medical/surgical benefits. Many therapeutic programs will work with insurance companies or may be able to direct to a third party to make sure that you receive the coverage you are entitled to.

Third-Party Lenders
Lenders can work with families to craft individualized payment plans.

GoFundMe
One of the world's largest social fundraising platforms to help people raise funds for personal, business, and charitable causes.

Web: *https://www.gofundme.com*

FAMILY SUPPORT

Private Coaching

For Parents, Adolescents, & Young Adults
Jonathan S. Mitchell, MA, LPC

Email: *jonathan.stein.mitchell@gmail.com*

For Parents
Nathan's Waypoint

Web: *https://www.nathanswaypoint.com*

SUPPORT ORGANIZATIONS

Al-Anon
A worldwide fellowship that offers a program of recovery for the families and friends of alcoholics, whether or not the alcoholic recognizes the existence of a drinking problem or seeks help.

Web: *https://al-anon.org*

Co-Dependents Anonymous (CoDA)
A program of recovery from codependence, to share experiences, strength, and hope in effort to find freedom where there has been bondage and peace where there has been turmoil in relationships with others.

Web: *https://coda.org*

Family Sanity
Resources in mental health for parents of teens and young adults.

Web: *https://www.familysanity.org*

NAMI: National Alliance on Mental Illness

Provides advocacy, education, support, and public awareness so that all individuals and families affected by mental illness can build better lives.

Web: *https://nami.org*

Parents of Addicted Loved Ones (PAL)

Provides hope through education and support to parents of adults dealing with substance use disorders. Free weekly meetings use an evidence-based curriculum designed specifically for parents by professionals in the treatment and recovery industry. Parents learn techniques to use when to trying to save a child from addiction, and suggestions on how to help them in a healthy way rather than enable their addiction. Not only are the physical and emotional health of parents improved, but in many cases their adult addicted loved one is led to seek recovery. Learn more and find a meeting near you on the website.

Web: *https://palgroup.org*

Warrior Families

A grassroots support group for parents who have children struggling with mental health issues. They offer Zoom support meetings and have a private member-only Facebook page. Chapters include Morris County, NJ; South Orange/Maplewood, NJ; and New York, NY.

Web: *https://warriorfamilies.org*

Willows in the Wind

Willows in the Wind offers peer to peer assistance to parents seeking support for their teen or young adult with behavioral, mental health, or substance abuse challenges.

Web: *https://www.willowsinthewind.com*

The Youth Mental Health Project

Provides parents and caregivers who are concerned about their children's mental health with informational resources and an opportunity, through its Parent Support Network, to find and support each other in a confidential and safe space. Regional affiliates of The Parent Support Network hold confidential and free parent support meetings which are run by volunteer, trained facilitators. Facilitators are parents with experience raising a child who has struggled with mental health. In addition, virtual meetings are available every week for parents residing anywhere in the United States.

Web: *https://ymhproject.org/parent-support-network*

MENTAL HEALTH AWARENESS AND ADDICTION PREVENTION

Choose Mental Health
The national voice for children's mental health. Through fundraising and awareness, making mental health okay to talk about, learn about, and ask questions about. Providing access and resources to families who don't know where to find them. Offering hope and solutions that are now available to everyone. Get help with your "next step."

Web: *https://choosementalhealth.org*

Erika's Lighthouse
Dedicated to educating and raising awareness about adolescent depression, encouraging good mental health, and breaking down the stigma surrounding mental health issues.

Web: *https://www.erikaslighthouse.org*

The Liv Project
A group of artists and filmmakers collaborating to create experiences, tools, and resources aimed at sparking the kind of fearless communication to help reverse the soaring rate of youth suicide and eliminate the stigma associated with mental health issues.

Web: *https://thelivproject.org*

Partnership to End Addiction
The nation's leading organization dedicated to addiction prevention and treatment recovery. Comprises a diverse community of researchers, advocates, clinicians, communicators, and more.

Web: *https://drugfree.org*

Song for Charlie

A family-run nonprofit charity dedicated to raising awareness about "fentapills"—fake pills made of fentanyl. Song for Charlie partners with experts, educators, parents, and other influencers to reach the most vulnerable group: young people between the ages of 13 through 30. Their programs highlight the emerging dangers of self-medication and casual drug use in the fentanyl era and encourage healthier strategies for coping with stress.

Web: *https://www.songforcharlie.org*

TWELVE QUESTIONS TO ASK BEFORE HIRING AN INDEPENDENT EDUCATIONAL CONSULTANT

1. Do you guarantee admission to a school, one of my top choices, or a certain minimum dollar value in scholarships? (Do NOT trust any offer of guarantees.)

2. How do you keep up with new trends, academic changes, and evolving campus cultures? How often do you get out and visit college, school, and program campuses, and meet with therapists, and admissions representatives? (The ONLY way to know about the best matches for you is to be out visiting schools regularly—we suggest IECs visit a minimum of 20 campuses per year.)

3. Do you belong to any professional associations? (NACAC and IECA are the two associations for independent educational consultants with established and rigorous standards for membership.)

4. Do you attend professional conferences or training workshops on a regular basis to keep up with regional and national trends and changes in the law?

5. Do you ever accept any form of compensation from a school, program, or company in exchange for placement or a referral? (They absolutely should not!)

6. Are all fees involved stated in writing, up front, indicating exactly what services I will receive for those fees?

7. Will you complete the application for admission, re-write my essays, or fill out the financial aid forms on my behalf? (No, they should NOT; it is essential that the student be in charge of the process and all materials should be a product of the student's own, best work.)

8. How long have you been in business as an independent educational consultant (IEC)?

9. What was your background prior to going into independent educational consulting? What was your training and education?

10. Will you use personal connections to get me into one of my top choices? (The answer should be NO. An IEC doesn't get you admitted—they help you to demonstrate why you deserve to be admitted.)

11. What specialized training do you have (LD, gifted, athletics, arts, etc.)?

12. Do you adhere to the ethical guidelines for private counseling established by IECA?

Questions are from the Independent Educational Consultants Association (IECA) website. Used with permission.

QUESTIONS TO ASK BEFORE MAKING A FINAL PLACEMENT SELECTION AT A RESIDENTIAL TREATMENT FACILITY

Admissions

What are your admissions criteria?

Who reviews my child's application? What are their credentials?

What are the costs? What do these costs cover?

Are there additional costs? If so, what are they?

How long will the admissions process take?

Who will I be meeting during the admissions process?

Licensing and Accreditation

Are you licensed by the state? What type of license is it? What state office issued the license?

Are you accredited by a mental health agency, such as Joint Commission (JCAHO), Council on Accreditation (COA), or Commission on Accreditation of Rehabilitation Facilities (CARF)?

Do you have a clinical director? What are their credentials? May I meet them?

What are the credentials of the staff members who will be working with my child? Specifically, what are the credentials of the counselors and therapists? Are they certified? Are they licensed within your state?

What organizations are you affiliated with?

Therapeutic Model/Clinical

Will my child be receiving clinical therapy? How often?

What will be expected of the parents during the program?

Do you provide family therapy?

Do you provide group therapy? If so, who facilitates it? Are there specific group therapies offered? (i.e., adoption issues, drug/alcohol abuse, etc.)

How is my child's progress judged? Who participates in determining my child's progress?

Academics

Do you provide an academic curriculum?

If so, what is the core curriculum?

Are you accredited by a national or regional accrediting agency? Is this accreditation through a third party? If so, what is their name?

Do you have teachers? If so, are they certified or licensed within your state?

How many students are in a class?

Is your academic curriculum internet/computer based?

Do you offer high school credits that can be transferred to other educational institutions?

Do you award high school diplomas?

Medication

Can my child be on medication while at your facility?

Who is responsible for the medication management? What are their credentials?

Where is the medication stored? Who has access to the medication?

Who administers the medication? What is their training?

Direct Care Staff

What type of training is provided to your direct care staff?

What are their duties and qualifications?

Do you perform background checks? Who does the background check? How extensive is it?

Do you provide ongoing training for your staff?

Risk Management

What measures do you have in place to keep my child safe?

What are your discipline procedures with resistant students?

How do you deal with risk-taking behaviors? (i.e., running away, self-harm, etc.)

Will my child be exposed to other students who have negative behaviors?

What if my child becomes ill? Do you have a nurse on staff? Will you transport my child to medical facilities?

Questions for Specific Program Types

Short Term Outdoor/Wilderness Program-Specific
How do you handle severe weather?

How do you handle emergencies?

What type of food do you provide?

How do you manage personal hygiene?

Long Term Residential-Specific
Are you a locked facility?

Is there 24-hour awake staff supervision?

How often will I see my child?

Will I be able to speak with my child on the telephone?

Will I be able to write and receive letters?

Success Rate / Outcomes
What is your success rate?

Do you administer an outcome study? If so, what is that data?

Do you have students return to your program?

Transition / Next Step
How many of your students return home after the program? If they don't return home, where do they go?

Will your program help us assess what is the next best step?

Will I need an educational consultant to plan a next step? Do you compensate an educational consultant for any reason?

Do you provide aftercare?

Questions are from the NATSAP website. Used with permission.

ENDNOTES

FOREWORD

By Jonathan S. Mitchell, MA, LPC
Therapist, Coach

INTRODUCTION

Inspiration for *A Wilderness Journey* overview: Winkler, Matthew. *What Makes a Hero?* (YouTube video) TED-Ed. 2012, December 12. https://www.youtube.com/watch?v=Hhk4N9A0oCA

Introduction to Joseph Campbell: Campbell, Joseph. *The Hero with a Thousand Faces.* (1949.) Reprint. 3d ed. Novato, CA: New World Library, 2008.

Modified twelve steps of the hero's journey: Vogler, Christopher. *The Writer's Journey: Mythic Structure for Writers.* 3d ed. Studio City, CA: Michael Wiese Productions, 2007.

Star Wars followed the hero's journey: Lee, Michael. "The Hero's Journey Breakdown: Star Wars." The Script Lab. 2019. https://thescriptlab.com/features/screenwriting-101/12309-the-heros-journey-breakdown-star-wars

Story pattern of the monomyth: "Hero's Journey 101: Definition and Step-by-Step Guide (With Checklist!)" reedsyblog. 2018. https://blog.reedsy.com/heros-journey

How the hero's journey relates to real life: Solomon, P. T. *Finding Joe.* (Short film available on YouTube) Balcony Releasing, 2011. https://www.youtube.com/watch?v=s8nFACrLxr0

OBH program compares Wilderness Therapy to the hero's journey: Hanselman, Jory. "The Hero's Journey." BaMidbar Wilderness Therapy. 2021. https://www.bamidbartherapy.org/the-heros-journey

Wilderness Therapy reflects the monomyth: "Wilderness Therapy: The Modern-Day Hero's Journey." New Vision Wilderness Therapy (website). 2020. https://beta.newvisionwilderness.com/wilderness-therapy-the-modern-day-heros-journey

Wilderness therapist relates recovery to the hero's journey: Reedy, Brad. "Recovery and the Hero's Journey." The Sober World. 2020. https://www.thesoberworld.com/2016/05/01/recovery-heros-journey

Definition of the hero's journey: "Hero's Journey." Wikipedia. 2021. https://en.wikipedia.org/wiki/Hero%27s_journey

Wilderness Therapy is an intervention: Russell, Keith, & John Hendee. "Wilderness Therapy as an Intervention and Treatment for Adolescents with Behavioral Problems." USDA Forest Service Proceedings RMRS-P-14. 2000. https://www.researchgate.net/publication/237722973_wilderness_therapy_as_an_intervention_and_treatment_for_adolescents_with_behavioral_problems

Definition of Wilderness Therapy: Russell, Keith. "What Is Wilderness Therapy?" Journal of Experiential Education 24, no. 2, 70–79. 2001. https://doi.org/10.1177/105382590102400203

Guide to Wilderness Therapy: Coley, Ryan, and Josh Watson. "Wilderness Therapy Programs: A Comprehensive Guide for Parents." Aspiro (website). 2021. https://aspiroadventure.com/wilderness-therapy-programs

Why Wilderness Therapy works: Burns, Patrick M. "Why Wilderness Therapy Works." Psychology Today (website). 2017. https://www.psychologytoday.com/us/blog/brainstorm/201712/why-wilderness-therapy-works

PHASE I: SEPARATION

Joseph Campbell quote: From Joseph Campbell's *Pathways to Bliss* Copyright © Joseph Campbell Foundation (jcf.org) 2004. Used with permission.

CHAPTER ONE: ORDINARY WORLD

Mental health epidemic: American Psychological Association. "Mental Health Issues Increased Significantly in Young Adults Over Last Decade: Shift May Be Due in Part to Rise of Digital Media, Study Suggests." *Science-Daily*. 15 March 2019. www.sciencedaily.com/releases/2019/03/190315110908.htm.

Dialectical Behavioral Therapy (DBT) workbook: Linehan, Marsha M. *Skills Training Handouts and Worksheets*. 2d ed. New York: The Guilford Press, 2015.

GeneSight: DNA medical testing: Genetic testing. GeneSight. (n.d.). https://genesight.com/

Individualized Education Program (IEP): "Understanding IEPs." Understood. 2021, April 28. https://www.understood.org/articles/en/understanding-individualized-education-programs

Weed can be addictive: "Is marijuana addictive?" NIDA. 2021, April 13. https://www.drugabuse.gov/publications/research-reports/marijuana/marijuana-addictive

Effects of weed on the developing brain: Weir, Kristen. "Marijuana and the Developing Brain." *American Psychological Association* 46, no. 10 (November 2015). https://www.apa.org/monitor/2015/11/marijuana-brain

Effects of weed on the developing brain: Shen, Helen. "Cannabis and the Adolescent Brain." Proceedings of the National Academy of Sciences of the United States of America (PNAS). January 7, 2020. https://www.pnas.org/content/117/1/7

Effects of weed on the developing brain: Morin, J.-F. G., M. H. Afzali, J. Bourque, S. H. Stewart, J. R. Séguin, M. O'Leary-Barrett, & P. J. Conrod (2019). "A Population-Based Analysis of the Relationship Between Substance Use and Adolescent Cognitive Development." *American Journal of Psychiatry* 176, no. 2, 98–106. https://doi.org/10.1176/appi.ajp.2018.18020202

Effects of weed on the developing brain: Paul, Marla. "Casual Marijuana Use Linked to Brain Abnormalities." 16 April 2014. https://news.northwestern.edu/stories/2014/04/casual-marijuana-use-linked-to-brain-abnormalities-in-students

Weed can trigger psychosis: Garey, Juliann. "Marijuana and Psychosis," Child Mind Institute (website). 2020, December 18. https://childmind.org/article/marijuana-and-psychosis

Illustrative analogy about weed addiction: *Marijuana Use and the Young-Adult Mind: A Response to New Research*. Oakwood Family Institute (website). (2014). https://oakwoodtreatment.com/?p=676

CHAPTER TWO: CALL TO ADVENTURE

The parent mentor (EC): Solochek, Canter & Associates. "Who We Are." 2018. https://thesc.group/

Why it's not advisable to trust negative reviews on residential programs: Beaton, Caroline. "Why You Can't Really Trust Negative Online Reviews." *The New York Times*. June 14, 2018. https://www.nytimes.com/2018/06/13/smarter-living/trust-negative-product-reviews.html

Study regarding whether online reviews reflect objective quality: Winer, Russell S., & Peter S. Fader. "Objective vs. Online Ratings: Are Low Correlations Unexpected and Does It Matter? A Commentary on de Langhe, Fernbach, & Lichtenstein." *Journal of Consumer Research* 42, no. 6. April 2016, pp. 846–849. https://academic.oup.com/jcr/article-abstract/42/6/846/2357889?redirectedFrom=fulltext

Family systems approach: "Family Involvement in Wilderness Therapy Programs." *Family Help & Wellness*. September 29, 2016. https://famhelp.com/bluefire-wilderness-therapy

Study on the family approach to treatment: Center for Substance Abuse Treatment. "Family Therapy." Chapter 6 in *Treatment of Adolescents with Substance Use Disorders*. (Treatment Improvement Protocol (TIP) Series, No. 32.) Rockville (MD): Substance Abuse and Mental Health Services Administration (US), 1999.
https://www.ncbi.nlm.nih.gov/books/NBK64343/

Transport: Lane, Bill. "What Is a Transport? Interview with Bill Lane." All Kinds of Therapy. Aug 7, 2015. Rev. 2021.
https://www.allkindsoftherapy.com/blog/what-is-a-transport--interview-with-bill-lane

CHAPTER FOUR: CROSSING THE THRESHOLD

Medicine wheel: "Medicine Ways: Traditional Healers and Healing: The Medicine Wheel and the Four Directions." Native Voices (website). (n.d.).
https://www.nlm.nih.gov/nativevoices/exhibition/healing-ways/medicine-ways/medicine-wheel.html

Medicine wheel: U.S. Department of the Interior. "The Medicine Wheel." U.S. National Parks Service. (n.d.).
https://www.nps.gov/articles/000/the-medicine-wheel.htm

Origin and meaning of the word mentor: Vogler, Christopher. *The Writer's Journey: Mythic Structure for Writers*. 3d ed. (p. 39). Studio City, CA: Michael Wiese Productions, 2007.

Definition of the word mentor: *Mentor*. (2012). Dictionary.com.
https://www.dictionary.com/browse/mentor

Family Systems Approach: Anita R. Tucker, Megan Paul, Jessalyn Hobson, Maggie Karoff, & Michael Gass. "Outdoor Behavioral Healthcare: Its Impact on Family Functioning," *NATSAP* 8, no. 1. 2016.
https://natsap.org/pdfs/jtsp/vol8/8_article_5.pdf

PHASE II INITIATION

Joseph Campbell quote: From Joseph Campbell's *The Hero with a Thousand Faces* Copyright © Joseph Campbell Foundation (jcf.org) 2008. Used with permission.

CHAPTER FIVE: SUPERNATURAL AIDS

Letter quote: Jewell, William. *The Golden Cabinet of True Treasure.* (1612.) Reprint. p. 167. Ann Arbor, MI: Text Creation Partnership, 2011. http://name.umdl.umich.edu/A04486.0001.001

Letter writing: Christenson, J. D., & A. L. Miller. "Slowing Down the Conversation: The Use of Letter Writing with Adolescents and Young Adults in Residential Settings." *Contemporary Family Therapy* 38, 23–31. 2016. https://doi.org/10.1007/s10591-015-9368-0

Job description of a wilderness therapist: *Wilderness Therapist Jobs.* JobMonkey. 2018, February 26. https://www.jobmonkey.com/uniquejobs5/wilderness-therapist

Field guide: Laskin, J. "What I Learned Working as a Wilderness Therapy Guide." Thrillist. (n.d.). https://www.thrillist.com/travel/nation/what-is-wilderness-therapy-programs-jobs-guide

Bow drill: Kirtley, Paul. "Succeed with Bow Drill!" Paul Kirtley, 2015. paulkirtley.co.uk/2011/bowdrill

Bow drill: Munilla, Robert. "Fire Starting with the Bow Drill." practicalsurvivor.com. (n.d.). http://www.practicalsurvivor.com/bowdrill

***I-feel* statements:** Rogerson, Beth. "The 5-Step Formula to Making Better 'I' Statements." Better Relating. 2015, June 8. https://bethrogerson.com/improve-communication

The Feelings Wheel: Willcox, Gloria. "The Feeling Wheel." *Transactional Analysis Journal* 12, 4, 274–276. (1982). https://www.tandfonline.com/doi/abs/10.1177/036215378201200411

Validation: Hall, Karen. "Understanding Validation: A Way to Communicate Acceptance." Psychology Today (website). April 26, 2012. https://www.psychologytoday.com/us/blog/pieces-mind/201204/understanding-validation-way-communicate-acceptance

Validation: Sorensen, Michael S. *I Hear You: The Surprisingly Simple Skill Behind Extraordinary Relationships.* Alpine, UT: Autumn Creek Press, 2017.

Mindfulness: Kornfield, Jack, and Daniel J. Siegel. *Mindfulness and the Brain.* Louisville, CO: Sounds True, 2010.

Three-part breath: Pizer, Ann. "How to Do Three-Part Breath (Dirga Pranayama) in Yoga." Verywell Fit. (n.d.). https://www.verywellfit.com/three-part-breath-dirga-pranayama-3566762

The SIFT technique: Siegel, Daniel J. *Brainstorm: The Power and Purpose of the Teenage Brain.* New York: Penguin Random House, 2015.

The SIFT technique: Siegel, Daniel J. "What Is SIFT, and How Can It Help with Parenting?" Kids in the House. 2014, June 11. https://www.kidsinthehouse.com/all-parents/health-and-wellness/brain-enrichment/what-sift-and-how-can-it-help-parenting

CHAPTER SIX: ROAD OF TRIALS

Stages of Grief: Kübler-Ross, Elisabeth, and David Kessler. *On Grief and Grieving.* (2004.) Reprint. New York: Scribner, 2014.

Neuropsychological testing and assessment: Corelli, Todd. "What Is Psychological Testing?" All Kinds of Therapy. 2019, October 31. https://www.allkindsoftherapy.com/blog/what-is-psychological-testing

Psychiatric medication in wilderness: Massey, Katie. "Research on Medication Changes in Wilderness Therapy." Evoke Therapy Programs. 2021. https://evoketherapy.com/resources/blog/katie-massey/research-on-medication-changes-in-wilderness-therapy

CHAPTER SEVEN: APPROACH TO THE INMOST CAVE

Difference between RTC and TBS: "What Is the Difference Between a Therapeutic Boarding School (TBS) and a Residential Treatment Center (RTC)? (Updated for 2018)." All Kinds of Therapy. 28 Oct. 2014. Rev. 2018. https://www.allkindsoftherapy.com/blog/the-difference-between-a-therapeutic-boarding-school-tbs-and-a-residential-treatment-

CHAPTER 8: ORDEAL

Quote: Jonathan S. Mitchell, MA, LPC (personal communication, June 2021).

Therapeutic implications of the solo: Wenzler, Fritz P. "Completing the Circle: The Mindset and Therapeutic Implications of the Wilderness Solo." Master's thesis, University of New Hampshire. 10 September 2020. https://scholars.unh.edu/cgi/viewcontent.cgi?article=1053&context=thesis

Solos: Naor, L., & O. Mayseless. "The Wilderness Solo Experience: A Unique Practice of Silence and Solitude for Personal Growth." *Frontiers in Psychology*. 10 September, 2020. https://doi.org/10.3389/fpsyg.2020.547067

CHAPTER NINE: ATONEMENT

Medicine wheel: "Medicine Ways: Traditional Healers and Healing: The Medicine Wheel and the Four Directions." Native Voices (website). (n.d.). https://www.nlm.nih.gov/nativevoices/exhibition/healing-ways/medicine-ways/medicine-wheel.html

Smudging: McCampbell, Harvest. *The Ancient Art of Smudging for Modern Times*. Summertown, TN: Native Voices, 2002.

PHASE III: RETURN

Joseph Campbell quote: From Joseph Campbell's *The Hero with a Thousand Faces* Copyright © Joseph Campbell Foundation (jcf.org) 2008. Used with permission.

CHAPTER TEN: SEIZING THE TREASURE

Cliff dwellings: U.S. Department of the Interior. "Mesa Verde National Park." U.S. National Parks Service. (n.d.). https://www.nps.gov/meve/index.htm

CHAPTER ELEVEN: ROAD TO AFTERCARE

Ninety days of darkness: Hana et al. "Field Guide Leah Dworkin Gives Us the Details on Wilderness Therapy." Love the Backcountry. 9 August, 2016. https://www.lovethebackcountry.com/field-guide-leah-dworkin-gives-us-details-wilderness-therapy

CHAPTER TWELVE: HERO'S RETURN

Transtheoretical Model: Prochaska, James O., and Carlo C. DiClemente. "Stages and Processes of Self-Change of Smoking: Toward an Integrative Model of Change." *Journal of Consulting and Clinical Psychology* 51, no. 3 (1983): 390–395. https://doi.org/10.1037/0022-006x.51.3.390

Stages of Change: Prochaska, James O., John C. Norcross, and Carlo C. DiClemente. *Changing for Good: The Revolutionary Program That Explains the Six Stages of Change and Teaches You How to Free Yourself from Bad Habits.* New York: Quill, 2007.

RESEARCH

Educational consultants (EC): Weld, Jake. "What Is an Educational Consultant, Therapeutic Consultant, or Placement Expert?" All Kinds of Therapy. 23 April 2015. https://www.allkindsoftherapy.com/blog/what-is-an-educational-consultant--therapeutic-consultant-or-placement-expert

SUBMARINES: Dr. Mike Gass (personal communication, June 30, 2021).

Wilderness Therapy theory: (Journal) Smithson, Sara. "The Theoretical Foundations of Wilderness Therapy." Master's thesis, Smith College. 2009. https://scholarworks.smith.edu/theses/1147

Podcast about Wilderness Therapy: White, Will. Podcast. Stories from the Field: Demystifying Wilderness Therapy. Podcast episode 130: "The Research at the Outdoor Behavioral Healthcare Center with Dr. Mike Gass." June 22, 2021. https://podcasts.apple.com/us/podcast/stories-from-the-field-demystifying-wilderness-therapy/id1440862416

Dr. Michael Gass: "Michael Gass." University of New Hampshire College of Health and Human Services. 2019, March 11. https://chhs.unh.edu/person/michael-gass

Adventure Therapy research at UNH: "UNH Receives Nearly $3 Million to Research Effectiveness of Wilderness Therapy." University of New Hampshire (website). 2021, March 2. https://www.unh.edu/unhtoday/news/release/2021/02/25/unh-receives-nearly-3-million-research-effectiveness-wilderness-therapy

Wilderness Therapy health benefits (Tent Treatment): White, Will. *Stories from the Field: A History of Wilderness Therapy.* pp. 6–7. Jackson, NH: Wilderness, 2015.

Wilderness Therapy health benefits: DeMille, S. M., & A. Tucker. "Body Composition Changes in an Outdoor Behavioral Healthcare Program." *Ecopsychology* 6, no. 3: 174–182. (2014). https://www.researchgate.net/publication/266137236_Body_Composition_Changes_in_an_Outdoor_Behavioral_Healthcare_Program

Metaphoric transfer in Adventure Therapy: Gass, M. A. "Enhancing Metaphor Development in Adventure Therapy Programs." *Journal of Experiential Education 14*, no. 2: 6–13. (1991). https://www.researchgate.net/publication/234636150_Enhancing_Metaphor_Development_in_Adventure_Therapy_Programs

Transfer of learning in Adventure Therapy: Gass, M. A. "Programming the Transfer of Learning in Adventure Education." *Journal of Experiential Education 8*, no. 3: 18–24. (1985). https://www.researchgate.net/publication/234660463_Programming_the_Transfer_of_Learning_in_Adventure_Education

Wilderness Therapy serves as a stabilizer: Quote by educational consultant Dr. Teri Solochek (personal communication, September 2020).

Wilderness Therapy is an intervention: Russell, Keith C., & John C. Hendee. "Wilderness Therapy as an Intervention and Treatment for Adolescents with Behavioral Problems." USDA Forest Service Proceedings RMRS-P-14. 2000. https://www.fs.fed.us/rm/pubs/rmrs_p014/rmrs_p014_136_141.pdf

Percentage of OBH students who go to aftercare vs. home: Dr. Mike Gass (personal communication, July 4, 2021).

Source of the adapted Common Path of Treatment flow chart: Case, Paul. *What Now? How Teen Therapeutic Programs Could Save Your Troubled Child.* p. 89. Franklin, TN: Common Thread Media, 2007.

Stages of Change in Wilderness Therapy: "How Do You Make Troubled Teens Change at Summit Achievement?" Summit Achievement. 2021. https://www.summitachievement.com/how-do-you-make-troubled-teens-change-at-summit-achievement

Stages of Change: Prochaska, J. O., C. C. DiClemente, & J. C. Norcross. "In Search of How People Change: Applications to Addictive Behaviors." *American Psychologist 47*, no. 9 (1992 Sept.): 1102–1114. https://pubmed.ncbi.nlm.nih.gov/1329589

Wilderness Therapy study on safety: Javorski, Stephen, & Michael Gass. "10-Year Incident Monitoring Trends in Outdoor Behavioral Healthcare: Lessons Learned and Future Directions." *Journal of Therapeutic Schools and Programs 6.* pp. 99–116. (2013). https://www.researchgate.net/publication/235678806_10-Year_Incident_Monitoring_Trends_in_Outdoor_Behavioral_Healthcare_Lessons_learned_and_future_directions

Wilderness Therapy study on safety: Outdoor Behavioral Healthcare Council. "OBH Is Safer Than Being at Home for the Average Teen." 2014. https://obhcouncil.com/research/obh-is-safer

Cost of Wilderness Therapy: "How Much Does Wilderness Therapy Cost?" All Kinds of Therapy. 2017, August 1. https://www.allkindsoftherapy.com/blog/how-much-does-wilderness-therapy-cost

Value of Outdoor Behavioral Healthcare: Gass, M., T. Wilson, B. Talbot, A. Tucker, M. Ugianskis, & N. Brennan. "The Value of Outdoor Behavioral Healthcare for Adolescent Substance Users with Comorbid Conditions." *Substance Abuse: Research and Treatment 13.* (2019). DOI: 10.1177/1178221819870768

Wilderness Therapy effectiveness: "UNH Research Finds Wilderness Therapy More Effective and Less Expensive." UNH Today. 2019, September 23. https://www.unh.edu/unhtoday/news/release/2019/09/24/unh-research-finds-wilderness-therapy-more-effective-and-less-expensive

Made in the USA
Monee, IL
04 March 2023

29167329R00135